Resources for
Addressing Faculty Bullying
in Higher Education

Libby Roderick, Editor

Kay Landis, Associate Editor

UNIVERSITY *of* ALASKA ANCHORAGE
Center for Advancing Faculty Excellence

Produced by
Center for Advancing Faculty Excellence
University of Alaska Anchorage
3211 Providence Drive
Anchorage, AK 99508

Published by
University of Alaska Anchorage

Original cover art and book design by David Freeman

ISBN: 978-0-9702845-4-9

Contributors

Libby Roderick
Associate Director, Center for Advancing Faculty Excellence
Director, Difficult Dialogues Initiative
University of Alaska Anchorage

Dr. Suzanne Burgoyne
Curators' Distinguished Teaching Professor of Theatre
Director, Center for Applied Theatre and Drama Research
University of Missouri

Dr. Andréa J. Onstad
Scriptwriter

Dr. E. J. R. David
Associate Professor, Psychology
Director, Alaska Native Community Advancement in Psychology Program
University of Alaska Anchorage

Dr. Osama Abaza
Professor, Civil Engineering
University of Alaska Anchorage

Shawnalee Whitney
Associate Professor, Journalism and Communication
Interim Director, Center for Advancing Faculty Excellence
University of Alaska Anchorage

Table of Contents

1: A Most Difficult Dialogue

2: Toxic Friday: the Video

3: Staging Toxic Friday On Your Campus

4: Faculty Reflections

5: Resources and Recommended Reading

Introduction

The Opportunity and the Challenge

Universities are—or should be—excellent venues for modeling civil discourse among people of differing perspectives, ideologies, and identities. At our best, academic communities demonstrate true democracy, treating one another with respect regardless of our differences.

Increasingly, however, institutions of higher education are coming to recognize how often we fail to live up to this ideal. Tales of toxic behavior in academic departments and other settings are legion. Cries for help go unanswered. When we leave it unchecked, chronic disrespectful behavior undermines our very essence, creates painfully high personal and institutional costs, and sends a message to our students and communities that we can't walk our talk as citizens of a civil society. Anything we can do to prevent or diminish this behavior—without jeopardizing the equally important values of academic freedom and freedom of speech—will benefit not just our faculty, but also our staff, students, administrators, and the wider communities we serve.

This book is a resource for faculty members, faculty developers, administrators, and other academic leaders who wish to address and prevent faculty-to-faculty bullying in higher education. It is accompanied by an online video, also called *Toxic Friday,* which uses a form of interactive theater to dramatically portray some of the most common toxic behaviors within academic departments. These materials are designed to serve as springboards for discussion, to help raise awareness of a complicated and pressing problem, and to encourage readers to identify and implement systemic solutions that create lasting change.

In these pages you will find a wide range of discussion materials, including context-setting ideas, discussion questions, and tips for facilitators, plus the complete *Toxic Friday* script for those who wish to stage their own live performances. We have included three very diverse faculty reflection essays in Part 4. The final section includes faculty recommendations, samples of policy language, and a selected bibliography of research materials and web resources.

We invite you to use *Toxic Friday* as a proactive resource to launch substantive discussions and to create culture changes that promote respectful, healthy, and safe interactions at all levels of higher education.

Active Bullying Situations

This book is a discussion resource, not a crisis manual. Acute situations need immediate solutions. If you are being actively bullied, contact your department chair, dean, or designated campus resource office.

Certain situations require special handling.

- **Violence and threats to personal safety.** If there is any concern that a situation could escalate into physical violence, contact appropriate resources on your campus (campus police or other specified agency) or dial 911 and involve your community's emergency response system.

- **Severe emotional distress.** The Americans with Disabilities Act (ADA) protects individuals who are suffering from severe emotional or mental distresses and traumas. Great care should be taken not to diagnose or otherwise label an individual's behavior. Contact your human resources office and follow your institution's protocol for ADA compliance. Document everything.

Be prepared.

- Encourage your campus communities to be proactive about prevention and systematic in response.
- Talk to your own experts: campus police, human resource offices, other sources of information and support.
- Consult web and print resources specific to active situations. See page 131 to get started.

1

A Most Difficult Dialogue

Faculty-to-Faculty Bullying
A Most Difficult Dialogue

By Libby Roderick

I have spent a good part of the past ten years helping university faculty learn to introduce and manage difficult dialogues in their classrooms. I've collaborated with dozens of talented educational leaders to design training intensives, support faculty learning communities, and present workshops to expand and deepen our skills at successfully engaging students on controversial topics. This work has taken me to campuses throughout the United States and twice to South Africa. In these forums, I have shared strategies for talking about racism, climate change, gun control, gay marriage, indigenous rights, and many other hot-button topics.

Libby Roderick is Associate Director of the Center for Advancing Faculty Excellence at the University of Alaska Anchorage (UAA). She directs UAA's Difficult Dialogues Initiative, serves as Vice President for the Difficult Dialogues National Resource Center, and consults with universities both nationally and internationally on related issues. She has co-authored and edited three faculty development handbooks: *Start Talking: A Handbook for Engaging Difficult Dialogues in Higher Education; Stop Talking: Indigenous Ways of Teaching and Learning and Difficult Dialogues in Higher Education*; and *Alaska Native Cultures and Issues: Response to Frequently Asked Questions*. In her spare time, she is an internationally recognized singer/songwriter and recording artist.

Faculty members are grateful for the support and offer extremely positive feedback. Nevertheless, one of the most frequent comments I hear is this: "Thanks for your help with difficult dialogues in the classroom, but that's not where things are the most difficult. Could you help me tackle conflicts with colleagues in my own department?"

Bullying in Academia

Do any of these people sound familiar? The colleague who repeatedly sends critical or even vicious emails and copies others both inside the department and beyond? The person who routinely shirks his or her share of the workload and then attacks others when they complain? The one who regularly comes late to department meetings, makes sarcastic comments, rolls his eyes, and poisons the atmosphere for discussion? The one who yells, excludes or withholds important information from certain colleagues, or sabotages a departmental program when she doesn't get her way?

Although the vast majority of faculty members display professional behavior most of the time, anyone who has worked in academia can point to many examples of bad behavior and to individuals who are known for chronically negative interactions. These individuals are found throughout the university community: students, staff, faculty, administrators, and parents of students. Their negative behaviors can be active or passive, major or mild, directed toward an individual or a group. While not illegal, these behaviors erode the sense of safety and respect necessary to maintain healthy learning and working communities. At the very least, they create distress for those around them. At worst, they produce hostile working environments and threaten personal safety.

The Workplace Bullying Institute (WBI) has been studying workplace bullying in general over the past decade, and their findings paint an alarming picture. A 2007 survey reported that workplace bullying is epidemic, a public health hazard, and disproportionately directed at women (Namie, 2007). A 2014 survey found bullies disproportionately target workers of color (Namie, 2014). Current anti-harassment laws rarely address bullying behaviors between individuals of the same gender or race, and many American employers ignore even the more obvious forms until they are forced to do so by a major incident or lawsuit. Perpetrators themselves usually suffer very little for their destructive behavior (Namie, 2007).

> *The person who bullied me befriended me at first. In time, however, things took an ugly turn. More than once, I was invited into his office for what seemed like a friendly conversation only to end up being berated for things I'd supposedly done that were 'hurting the department.' I began to doubt my own judgment. Eventually I became nervous in conversations with other colleagues and unsure about how I should interact with students.*
>
> — Associate Professor

Other researchers suggest that bullying is on the rise in academia as well (Cipriano, 2011; Twale & DeLuca, 2008). However, because academics have paid "little systematic empirical research attention" to bullying in academic settings specifically (Keashly & Neuman, 2010), it is difficult to determine if bullying is actually increasing or if it is only being more systematically reported or taken more seriously. Either way, researchers are placing an increased focus on it as an issue of concern. A number of papers, articles, and books have been published in recent years speaking to the problem (see our selected Bibliography, beginning on page 126). *The Chronicle of Higher Education* has published several articles (Fogg, 2008; Gravois, 2006), and lively discussions are also taking place in less formal settings, such as private conversations and online blogs.

The data we do have points to the scope of the problem. In one study, approximately 62% of higher education employees reported having experienced bullying at least once (Hollis, 2012). In another, 32% of university employees and 49% of faculty members reported bullying that lasted longer than three years (Keashly & Neuman, 2008).

In nationwide surveys of department chairs, 59% reported dealing with "noncollegial, uncivil faculty," and 73% indicated that collegiality should be a fourth criteria (in addition to teaching, research, and service) for tenure decisions (Cipriano, 2011). A 2012 faculty and staff survey at my own university revealed numerous experiences with individuals who create hostile work environments through bullying or other toxic behaviors; respondents indicated a strong desire to have the institution intervene more forcefully in these situations (University of Alaska Anchorage, 2012).

Many forms of bullying are linked to questions of diversity, inclusivity, and equity within our faculty ranks. As Dr. E.J.R. David points out later in this book (see page 91), inequities in the academy mirror inequities in society at large. Evidence suggests that faculty members from socially marginalized groups such as women, African Americans, people with disabilities, and members of the lesbian, gay, bisexual, transgender, and queer communities are more likely to be targeted by bullying behaviors (Hollis, 2012; Namie, 2014; Lampman, 2012). Understandably, they may respond with greater distress than others who don't share their social and political vulnerabilities (Lampman et al., 2009).

> *She was smart enough to make me look like the guilty one. She would take an email I wrote her, edit it to sound bad, and send it to everyone in the department. She would mock me in meetings and say untrue and unflattering things about me to others. The attacks never stopped. Later, she began attacking others in my department the same way. Sadly, it was a relief to know that some of my colleagues had similar experiences and could understand. But it didn't stop the fear.*
>
> — Tenured Associate Professor

Many faculty members enter the academy having already endured years or even decades of oppressive experiences. Bullying can serve to reinforce this charged history, leading some to drop out of the academy altogether. An institution's lack of commitment to diversity issues in general may discourage faculty members from reporting their experiences and prevent the institution from providing adequate responses. For these and other reasons, it is critical to consider identity dynamics in all discussions of bullying in academia.

Definitions and Gray Areas

There is no universal agreement about precisely what we mean by terms like *incivility, uncollegiality, bullying,* or *toxic behavior.* Nor are there clear lines where one shades into the other. We have used these terms more or less interchangeably throughout this book because we didn't want to limit the scope of discussion by narrowing our focus too tightly. Instead, we encourage readers to wrestle with these questions themselves and to work with others at their institutions to create their own definitions, draw their own lines, and focus their attention on the most pressing problems in their individual environments.

Lacking legal criteria, it is up to us to decide where to draw the line between relatively minor forms of incivility (the "merely" annoying or offensive) and unacceptable behaviors that are threatening or damaging to others. Faculty members have a right to free speech and must sometimes simply be "allowed to be a jerk," as one of them put it in a recent discussion on our campus. Academic freedom gives faculty members the right to engage in intense intellectual disagreement, to express offensive ideas, and to research and teach both what and how they choose. Steps taken to ensure safe working environments should not threaten or damage these freedoms in any way.

> *The bully in our department created a completely toxic environment. Almost all of us had been targets at one point or another, so we were always walking on eggshells. No one at higher levels seemed willing or able to help resolve the problem. It got to a point where I dreaded department meetings and other time in the office. It was very isolating.*
>
> — Tenured Associate Professor

However, what should we do when individuals cross the line into behaviors that are harmful to coworkers and students? Bullying and certain other forms of incivility and toxic behavior clearly cross that line by interfering with others' rights to self-expression and safety in the workplace. Cumulatively, certain behaviors create a hostile work environment for others.

A growing body of work is closing in on some common parameters for thinking and talking about these behaviors. Most definitions of incivility or bullying include active behaviors such as gossiping, insulting, yelling, swearing, damaging property, and otherwise disrupting civil discourse and work activities. They also include passive behaviors such as withholding critical information, assigning unfair workloads, and systematically ignoring, dismissing, or excluding people from important events. Virtually all distinguish between a single or small number of negative interactions (anyone can have a bad day) and a consistent pattern of incivility over time that produces ongoing negative effects on others in the work environment. Most definitions include electronic or written behaviors as well as physical or verbal ones.

This wide swath encompasses an enormous gray area of damaging, yet still legal, behaviors. Each institution must wrestle with where a particular set of behaviors falls within that gray area, and how it can or should respond.

Dimensions of Toxic Behavior: Types and Levels

Various researchers and task forces have identified the following types of incivility or bullying:

Classic bullying, which occurs when a person with greater power intimidates or bullies someone with lesser power. The Workplace Bullying Survey concludes that "the stereotype is real: 72% of all bullies are bosses" (Namie, 2007).

14

Contrapower harassment, the reverse of classic bullying, in which a person with lesser power harasses a person with greater power, such as when a student harasses a faculty member. Studies by UAA Professor Dr. Claudia Lampman report that women, untenured faculty, younger faculty, and faculty of color tend to be the most frequent targets and that women tend to suffer the most negative impacts of these behaviors (Lampman et al., 2009; Lampman, 2012).

Colleague-to-colleague bullying, as when a person uses destructive behavior against someone with roughly equal power. A study of faculty experience by Keashly and Neuman (2008) reports, "Colleagues were more likely to be identified as bullies by faculty (63.4%), while superiors were more likely to be identified as bullies by frontline staff (52.9%)." Faculty concern about workplace harassment was more likely to be associated with colleagues (especially senior colleagues) and superiors than with students. The *Toxic Friday* project speaks primarily to this type of bullying.

Mobbing, as when two or more people gang up on an individual. (The term is credited to industrial psychologist Dr. Heinz Leymann.) In the Keashly and Neuman study (2008), "faculty members were almost twice as likely as staff to report being the victims of mobbing by three or more actors (14.5% vs. 8% respectively)."

Conspicuous exclusion or isolation, which has the effect of harming another person's reputation in the workplace or hindering another person's work.

Sabotage, which can be directed toward an academic program, an initiative, or someone else's work. These acts include purposely passing over qualified candidates in favor of a decision-maker's friends and other forms of interference that limit an individual's capacity for academic expression.

Abuse of authority, such as using threats or retaliation in exercising authority, supervision, or guidance, or impeding another person from exercising shared governance rights, etc.

> *He was truly a Dr. Jekyll and Mr. Hyde. He appeared to be smooth and even kind, and then you'd realize he was talking about sabotaging someone else's sabbatical proposal. I would find myself agreeing with him and only later realize that he had talked me into doing something damaging to another colleague. As odd as it may seem, I was totally afraid to argue against him.*
>
> — Tenured Associate Professor

Administrative incivility, including systematic budget manipulation, lack of transparency, structural misalignment, and chronic failure of the institution's leaders to provide accurate information. These behaviors are discussed at some length in Cipriano's *Facilitating a Collegial Department in Higher Education* (2011).

Another dimension to consider is the level of severity: How much damage can or does the behavior cause?

Offensive behaviors, such as insulting or abusive language, shouting, swearing, mocking, derogatory remarks, and epithets may be the mildest forms of incivility, but they can still cause damage. The University of Wisconsin Madison faculty anti-bullying policy specifies behaviors that fall "outside the range of commonly accepted expressions of disagreement, disapproval, or critique in an academic culture and professional setting that respects free expression."

Hostile behaviors, such as threats, intimidation, humiliation, unwanted physical contact, vandalism, property damage, and invasion of personal space ratchet up the damage potential significantly. These behaviors do not have to rise to an illegal level to be harmful in the workplace.

Violent behaviors provide a direct threat to personal safety or the safety of others. Any threat of violence moves the questionable behavior beyond bullying and into a category of its own.

> *In the beginning, she trusted me enough to share with me her real opinion of deans or colleagues. She would call them ugly names and say awful things and talk about her plans to thwart their efforts or damage their careers. In person, however, she would flirt with them to get what she wanted. She was attractive, so some of the male administrators wanted her attention. It made me realize how incredibly manipulative she was.*
>
> — Tenured Associate Professor

Working Policies and Definitions

In the absence of a universally accepted definition, universities and researchers are writing their own definitions and creating policies to meet their individual challenges. Here are a few examples to help launch conversations about how bullying may be better defined on your own campus. Other examples are included in Part 5.

Researcher Macgorine Cassell (2011) separates bullying behavior into one of three categories:
- inaction (e.g. withholding praise, feedback or information; delaying important actions);
- subtle action (e.g. hostile glaring; interrupting; eye-rolling); and
- action (e.g., rude/disrespectful behavior; shouting; humiliation).

An Eastern Washington University task force (2010) specifies unacceptable behaviors as
- intentional;
- targeted at an individual or group;
- repeated;
- hostile or offensive; and
- creating an intimidating or threatening environment with risk of physical or psychological harm.

An Oregon State University policy (2013) emphasizes the victim's experience, defining bullying as conduct that would cause a reasonable person in the victim's position substantial emotional distress and undermine his or her ability to work, study, or participate in regular life activities or the activities of the university.

A University of Wisconsin Madison policy (2014) recognizes impacts on the workplace and the victim, labeling unacceptable behaviors as those that do not further the university's academic or operational interests, that make work conditions inhospitable, and that impair another person's ability to carry out his/her responsibilities to the university.

Special Features of Academic Culture

However we define them, incivility and toxic behaviors are neither unique nor exclusive to academia; they are, in fact, among humanity's most vexing problems. From playground bullies to global extremists and terrorists, questions about what should be done and who has the responsibility to take appropriate action command considerable attention at all levels in our society. As others have said, it's not a higher education problem—it's a people problem.

Still, academic cultures do have several unique structures and practices that can increase the likelihood of colleague-to-colleague incivility.

> *No one believed me. Everyone asked what I did to set her off. I didn't do anything but disagree with her, but that was enough to get on her attack list.*
>
> — Tenured Associate Professor

Tenure
On the one hand, tenure provides some extremely important protections, allowing faculty members to speak out about bullying and many other issues with less fear of retaliation. On the other hand, tenure can lead to a false sense of invulnerability that permits some faculty members to act irresponsibly. Courts have repeatedly found that tenure is not a protection in cases where a faculty member represents a threat to his or her colleagues.

Tenure can also result in very long-term relationships between and amongst faculty and staff members, which can lead to long-term bullying. One report found that 21% of its sample had experienced bullying that had persisted for more than five years, and nearly half the faculty respondents had experienced it for more than three years (McKay et al., 2008 in Keashly & Neuman, 2010). The researchers concluded, "It may be that academia is a particularly vulnerable setting for such persistent aggression."

Evaluation practices

Many researchers point out that our most common academic evaluation practices can foster widespread feelings of injustice, unfairness, and mistrust. "Faculty members are evaluated using subjective, often ambiguous, criteria," say Greenberg and Colquitt (2005), who reviewed evaluations of scholarly and intellectual contributions, department- and college-wide service, continuing growth, and community service. "Few institutions have clear standards for judging such contributions and, instead, rely on general guidelines or descriptive criteria." Judgments made in this manner often lead to "perceptions of distributive injustice, unfair treatment associated with outcomes and procedural injustice, and unfair treatment associated with the decision-making process used to determine those outcomes."

The peer review process complicates matters even further. "Hidden agendas can abound," say Higgerson and Joyce (2007), most notably at "the departmental level, where people have 'histories' with each other and are often in competition for scarce resources (money, equipment, space, power, high-caliber students, etc.)."

> *Departmental bullying is like domestic abuse. You're in these relationships for a long, long time. When things go wrong, other people know about it. Your colleagues down the hall are like the neighbors who stay silent even when they hear yelling in the next apartment. They might give you a sympathetic look or a kind word at the copy machine, but no one seems to have a way to change the situation.*
>
> — Associate Professor

Academic freedom

Some individuals confuse the concept of academic freedom with the right to behave and speak in any way they choose. An excellent summary by the President of the American Association of University Professors cites twelve rights and freedoms the concept guarantees, including the right to engage in intellectual debate without fear of censorship or retaliation, and the right to express one's views—in speech, writing, and through electronic communication, both on and off campus—without fear of sanction *unless the manner of expression substantially impairs the rights of others* (emphasis added). The summary goes on to enumerate twelve things the protections do not cover. Academic freedom does not mean a faculty member can "harass, threaten, intimidate, ridicule, or impose his or her views" on others, nor does it guarantee lifetime employment or protect incompetent or dishonest teachers from losing their jobs (Nelson, 2010).

We can exercise academic freedom and free speech and disagree with one another's ideas (sometimes passionately) while still behaving in ways that are respectful of one another. This is the essence of a healthy democracy as well as a healthy university culture. As Yale's former president Kingman Brewster once put it, "Universities should be safe havens where ruthless examination of realities will not be distorted by the aim to please or inhibited by the risk of displeasure." However, he also said, "We must never let disagreement fester into disrespect" (Lassila, 2016).

Some are wary that administrators will use the charge of incivility as an excuse for "stifling dissent and unorthodox speech and thought" (Donald Downs, quoted in Schneider, 2015). Behavior-based assessment matrices (such as those described on page 125) were developed as one way of ensuring that charges of incivility are grounded in objective evidence. Substantive faculty discussions can identify other ways as well.

Celebration of critical thought

The academic world sees criticism as part of the routine work of a scholarly community. Critiquing each other's ideas is what academics do. However, the process often takes a vicious turn, especially in conference settings, when scholars attack work in ways that denigrate the author instead of constructively challenging the scholarship. In some cases, nasty criticism may even increase a scholar's reputation for "cleverness," which one blog calls "a form of currency in academia" (thesiswhisperer.com).

> *I was driving home when I heard the report about that professor in Alabama who gunned down her colleagues in a department meeting. I pulled over, shaking and sick to my stomach. The bully in our department had been raging and red-faced in department meetings and had sabotaged both programs and people. Were we headed down a similar path?*
>
> — Associate Professor

Given the importance placed on one's "accomplishments, intellectual rigor, and reputation," say Keashly and Neuman (2010), it is understandable that the bullying behaviors most frequently cited in academia involve forms of isolation, threats to professional status, and acts that obstruct the target's professional goals. Weapons of choice include behaviors that undermine a colleague's professional standing, authority, and competence, or that impede access to key resources for his or her work. "Within the academic culture of reasoned discussion and debate, such behaviors can be justified by the bully as normative…that is, part of the 'cut and thrust' of academic discourse," say Nelson & Lambert (quoted in Keashly & Neuman, 2010).

Power imbalances, scarcity, and other factors

Some toxic behaviors may stem from the culture of scarcity, in which scholars perceive themselves to be (and often actually are) competing for limited resources to support their research and/or teaching. Others are the result of power imbalances between faculty groups. Junior and untenured faculty members often feel too vulnerable to protest if bullied by senior faculty members; adjuncts and other contingent faculty feel much the same with respect to full-time faculty, no matter how junior. Both groups may feel disempowered in relation to administrators. And when academic leaders are largely drawn from a base of peers, faculty members may be reluctant to intervene in the behavior of their former peers or those who will be in a position to evaluate them once the leadership position rotates.

A number of researchers have called attention to the increasing stresses associated with employment in higher education in recent decades (Gillespie et al, 2001). A non-exhaustive list (Oxenford & Kuhlenschmidt, 2011) includes:

- increased workloads and higher accountability demands;
- ambiguous tenure and promotion standards;
- increased competition for grants, publications, and positions;
- high stakes peer assessments and public criticism;
- unsupportive administrators and reduced autonomy;
- fiscal pressures such as reduced funding, salary freezes, furloughs, and delayed retirement;
- expectations of independent work and sole authorship;
- increased research and publication pressures; and
- increased work-home conflict due to work pressures.

Personal and Institutional Costs

Even a single instance of true faculty-to-faculty bullying comes with extraordinary costs on every level: individual, departmental, and institutional. As Jeffery Buller (2006) says, "Every department chair understands the importance of promoting collegiality within his or her department. Few factors can bring the productivity of a department to a standstill and destroy its reputation as quickly as can the presence of even a single uncollegial faculty member."

> *After seeing how the dean and others handled my complaint, I felt minimized and isolated. I withdrew from my colleagues, avoided meetings, and turned down requests for new projects and collaborations.*
>
> — Tenured Full Professor

Damage to individuals can take physical, psychological, and emotional forms ranging from stress and depression to sleep disturbances, phobias, and musculoskeletal or digestive problems (Von Bergen, 2006). In a Workplace Bullying Institute survey, 45% of bullying victims reported negative impacts on health; a third of these indicated impacts lasting more than a year (Namie, 2007).

A report from the Safety and Health Assessment and Research for Prevention program in the state of Washington (2011) lists the following consequences of bullying:

- high stress levels;
- psychological and/or physical symptoms;
- diminished work performance (with lasting impacts on a faculty member's career);
- deep feelings of isolation and lack of support;
- irritability and reactivity;
- additional tensions at home and with family members;
- a need to seek personal counseling, sometimes at great financial costs;
- a decision to leave the university and/or academia; and
- ongoing primary or secondary trauma.

Damage to departments and institutions includes destructive political behavior, lack of cooperation, interpersonal aggression, withdrawal behavior, lowered organizational commitment, and sabotage. Of particular relevance to discussions of bullying among faculty is the impact on job satisfaction, productivity, performance, and turnover (Keashly & Neuman, 2010). The effects often spill over onto staff, students, and colleagues in other departments.

Abusive work situations create measurable institutional costs, including increases in medical and workers' compensation claims, lawsuits, high turnover, absenteeism, poor customer relationships, and acts of sabotage and revenge (Stone, 2009). Von Bergen (2006) identifies faculty bullying as the source of "lost efficiency, absenteeism, sick leave due to stress-related illnesses, high staff turnover, severance packages, law suits, self-defensive paperwork, and wasted time at work involving targets defending themselves and networking for support. In extreme cases, violence may be the tragic result of workplace bullying."

> *Bullying took a terrible toll on my health. I had stress-related health problems, saw a counselor for a time, and even needed dental work because I was clenching my teeth until my molars cracked. My out-of-pocket costs were sizable. It made me feel even worse that the school would rather let my health suffer than deal with the problem.*
>
> — Associate Professor

Focus on Faculty

Toxic Friday was designed to help launch faculty discussions about appropriate responses to faculty misbehavior. We contend that faculty members can and must play leading roles in determining how best to ensure the health and safety of their own academic departments. In our experience, faculty-driven problems are best addressed by faculty-driven solutions.

Preventing or taking steps to end incivility, however, will require a systemic response. Bullying doesn't stop until there is an environmental or cultural change within the organization, so people at every level feel both empowered and equipped to speak up and to intervene appropriately. Faculty, staff, and students must be supported to speak frankly; administrators, human resources staff, and union representatives must be prepared to take corrective action when necessary. Policies and response protocols must be clear, widely distributed and understood, and reliably enforced for individuals at every level.

Other constituencies such as staff, students, administrators, union personnel, and human resources personnel can and should be involved in these discussions. To truly ensure a healthy working and learning community, populations throughout the university need to hold similar discussions about behaviors within their own groups. Although the *Toxic Friday* materials target the faculty experience, we hope they can serve as models for discussions among other groups as well.

Towards a Better Future

Like all forms of bullying, the faculty-to-faculty variety is a thorny problem. Solving it will require that all members of university communities—administrators, faculty, staff, students, and university supporters—come together to craft and agree on systemic solutions that respect academic freedom, freedom of speech, and intellectual, personal, and cultural diversity, while simultaneously ensuring that everyone on our campuses is safe from all forms of violence. We hope that the resources and insights offered here will stimulate productive discussions and move our campuses that much closer to a future in which all community members are honored and our highest values are lived every day.

2

Toxic Friday: The Video

Viewing the Video

Toxic Friday is a video presentation of an interactive theater piece that showcases several forms of intimidation, bullying, and other toxic behaviors frequently reported as common within academic departments. The video contains three major elements:

1) a scripted performance, dramatizing one Friday morning in an imaginary American Studies department;

2) an excerpt from a *talk-back session*, in which the actors remain in character and respond to questions from a live audience; and

3) six individual scenes from the performance which allow for targeted discussion about the issues raised in each.

The characters are fictional composites, but their situations and interactions are based on the real experiences of many faculty members we interviewed. The scenarios are informed by our research and faculty interviews, which told us that these situations—and others both more and less subtle—are disturbingly common in the academic world.

This video is a tool to help faculty members (and others) develop a shared picture of what faculty-to-faculty bullying looks like, and begin to take steps toward the culture change necessary to create safer, healthier academic institutions. Suggested discussion questions and activities begin on page 34.

 Watch the Video
http://www.difficultdialoguesuaa.org/toxicfriday/
Username: toxicfriday
Password: t0xiC*!#

Using Interactive Theater to Start the Conversation

By Libby Roderick

The *Toxic Friday* video is based on an interactive theater script developed in the spring of 2014 at the University of Alaska Anchorage (UAA). Interactive (or applied) theater is a particularly useful strategy for engaging in dialogues on difficult topics in ways that illuminate dynamics that might otherwise remain invisible and for breaking through intellectual roadblocks that can inhibit actual change. Scripted from real situations and people, actors play fictional characters to dramatize events, allowing audience members to relate to the situations without feeling exposed as participants. It is uniquely suited to stimulating productive discussions while protecting anonymity. The highly charged and complex issue of faculty-to-faculty bullying is, obviously, an excellent focus for this kind of work.

An interactive theater event usually consists of three parts: a scripted performance, a *talk-back session*, and several opportunities for audience members to intervene. The first part resembles a traditional theater performance, with actors playing fictional characters in scripted interactions while the audience merely watches. In the second part, the actors remain in character after the performance and the audience is invited to engage with them. Audience members can ask questions, confront characters about their behaviors, and explore invisible layers beneath surface behaviors such as the characters' hidden circumstances and motivations. In the third stage, audience members are invited to intervene by improvising alternate responses and interactions with the actors, trying out solutions that may have occurred to them during the performance. Actors prepare for these interactive and improvisational sessions by creating detailed backstories for their characters and identifying talking points to reveal through their responses. Audience members are prepared through warm-up exercises and other information presented by the director and/or facilitator.

I witnessed several interactive theater workshops with a Difficult Dialogues colleague of mine, Dr. Suzanne Burgoyne, at the University of Missouri (UM). Her work with the UM Interactive Theatre Troupe (ITT) demonstrated how effectively this technique could help faculty tackle issues of power, privilege, and identity in the classroom and beyond.

At UAA, we performed UM's interactive script *A Knock at the Door* for a faculty audience in 2014, using local actors to explore unconscious biases in faculty hiring practices. Our faculty attendees watched actors portray common search committee interactions and attitudes without having to put anyone (including themselves) on the spot. Those who felt they had witnessed or been the targets of discrimination could point to its occurrence in the performance (rather than in their own experience). Others who may have unconsciously perpetuated discriminatory attitudes or behaviors could hear these things being discussed and reflect privately on their own behaviors without feeling a need to defend themselves in front of their colleagues. With this strategy, we were able to hold substantive discussions about biases in the search process and identify steps we need to take to eliminate them.

Script Development

Fortunately, Dr. Burgoyne was willing to help us on the Toxic Friday project as well. She put us in touch with playwright Dr. Andréa J. Onstad, author of *A Knock at the Door*, whom we hired to write a new script for us on the topic of academic incivility and bullying.

The script Dr. Onstad created (beginning on page 49) was both thoroughly researched and deeply collaborative. She began by reviewing the literature on academic bullying and workplace bullying in general. From there, she developed an extensive set of interview questions and conducted personal interviews with faculty members, union representatives, and human resource personnel at UAA, the University of Missouri, and the University of Texas at Austin. The interview subjects were asked how they would define bullying and what experiences they had had. They were also guaranteed anonymity. No one but the playwright ever heard the participants' words or stories.

After the interviews, the playwright collaborated with local rehearsal director Dr. Gabrielle Barnett by providing bullying scenarios and language from her research to develop improvisations for the actors. She was looking for situations that best illustrated the array of experiences she'd uncovered and that gave the actors the greatest range of dramatic possibilities. The improvisation rehearsals were recorded and transcribed, adding another layer of raw material and a wider range of perspectives to the process.

Eventually, Dr. Onstad sat down with a foot-high stack of transcripts and notes to develop the first working drafts of the script. She focused on key phrases, recurring situations, and personal anecdotes that she could translate theatrically. She identified common behaviors that seemed to be creating the most difficulty: sending malicious emails, invading personal space, and yelling. She also identified responses to those behaviors, from colleagues looking the other way to administrators lacking specific training or protocols to follow. She paid attention to reports about patterns in nonverbal reactions as well, from eye rolling and staring to withdrawing into a cell phone.

Since interactive theater is meant to draw audiences into participating, the characters are written so that they make mistakes. Each mistake is an opportunity for an audience member to jump in and try to change things or suggest solutions that might lead to different outcomes. "From my research," says Dr. Onstad, "I deemed it important that victims as well as bullies see themselves in the roles they play. The point is not for me to resolve the bullying problem of the play, but to create moments that might prompt an audience member to take action to change the outcome."

As drafts evolved, faculty members were invited to comment on run-throughs. Their responses, wide ranging and often contradictory about the same behavior or scene, were duly noted and recorded:

- "This part really resonates with my experience, but that other part is completely unrealistic. It would never happen."
- "Are you kidding!? That happens in my department all the time!"
- "Oh, that behavior is so exaggerated. You've got to take it out or tone it down; it's just too extreme."
- "That's *nothing* compared to what I'm dealing with."

In summarizing this extensive and collaborative development process, the playwright concluded, "It's important to point out that I chose generic bullying situations rather than specific examples from the UAA interviews. I continue to honor anonymity, and I always will. However, I want to stress that every single bullying incident included in the final script happened somewhere at some time."

Performance and Discussion

After months of research, development, and rehearsal, we were finally ready for our first performances and discussions. The events were produced by the Center for Advancing Faculty Excellence (CAFE), UAA's faculty development center. The staging was very basic: a few desks, chairs, and simple props such as laptops, briefcases, and books, including a copy of *Robert's Rules of Order*. The production was funded through the Provost's office and United Academics, UAA's largest faculty union. I served as host and discussion facilitator.

At the beginning of each event, I took time to introduce the concept of interactive theater and to contextualize the performance with a slide presentation that included sample definitions, statistics, our university's existing policies and procedures, and a few examples of anti-bullying policies from other universities and sources. Suggestions for this background material begin on page 31.

The performance itself was introduced by Dr. Barnett, who also moderated the talk-back session afterward. Audiences asked questions such as, "Why did you take (or fail to take) that action?" and, "What were you thinking when you did such and so?" The actors could respond in either *timed-in mode* (a public response, with all the other characters able to overhear and challenge them) or *timed-out mode* (a private response, as if no other character could hear). For example, an audience member might ask a character why she did not do more to stand up for her colleagues. Publicly, the character might say she believes it's the role of the department chair—not the faculty member—to intervene. Privately, she might reveal that she is close to retirement and just doesn't have the energy to engage in departmental conflicts anymore. Each talk-back session was necessarily unique, as the questions, audiences, and sometimes even the cast differed from performance to performance.

For reasons of both time and audience comfort, we chose not to include audience-improvised interventions in our events. Instead, after the talk-back session, I opened things up for a facilitated discussion on the issues raised. Over and over again, I emphasized the need for confidentiality and reminded participants not to identify any individual within our institutions as either a bully or a victim.

We held five live performances and discussions of *Toxic Friday* throughout the 2014-15 academic year. Some performances were presented to discrete groups of faculty members or administrators only; others were presented to mixed groups that included faculty, administrators, union representatives, and human resources staff. We found that the discrete group discussions provided greater freedom to speak about incivility within the group; mixed group discussions helped promote collaborative movement towards systemic solutions.

The final performance was filmed in UAA's Journalism Television Studio to create the video that accompanies this book.

Tips for Discussion Facilitators

The role of the discussion facilitator is critical in creating productive conversations.

Set the Context

Audiences should be given enough background information to have an informed discussion. We recommend that the facilitator take a few minutes either before or after the performance or video to introduce some or all of the following topics:
- what we mean by *faculty bullying*, with a few definitions and examples;
- why this issue matters, including costs to individuals and institutions;
- unique features of academia that tend to protect or even promote bullying;
- existing policies and procedures at their institution;
- institutional resources to support individuals currently in active bullying situations;
- sample policies, procedures, and resources from other institutions or sources; and
- possible steps their institution might take.

      With the exception of institution-specific materials, these topics are all covered throughout this book.

Orient the Audience to Unique Features of Interactive Theater

Our discussion facilitator always included some version of the following advice:
- Most of us are used to looking at theater as entertainment, catharsis, or a glimpse into the human condition. Interactive theater is a bit more charged. The performance is deliberately dramatic, and the plot is left intentionally unresolved. The idea is to stimulate conversation on a sensitive subject. Please do not judge it on the basis of the kind of theater you may see in a playhouse.
- This performance portrays only one out of many possible scenarios. There are many different types of bullying and many different departmental cultures. The video focuses on a single, albeit common, scenario. We recognize that you may have a very different experience, and we encourage you to talk about that during the discussion that follows the performance.
- This performance also involves a specific cast. Please consider how the dynamics might differ with a different cast (i.e., with the roles played by actors of different genders, racial/ethnic identities, countries of origin, ages, and so on).

- The precise behaviors highlighted in this performance may not occur in your department, or you may identify with only a single element of them. We know they are common because they came up in interviews with faculty members from three different universities. Even if you are fortunate enough never to have experienced any of them, we ask you to please keep an open mind. These behaviors may occur in other departments in your institution, and one or more of your colleagues may have experienced—or be experiencing—them.
- *Toxic Friday* is designed to demonstrate and highlight problems related to bullying throughout the university system (deans, chairs, departmental colleagues, unions, human resource offices, etc.). Please don't take any of the portrayals personally (unless the shoe fits!).
- If viewing *Toxic Friday* and/or participating in the discussion is distressing in any way, the following university resources are available to support you. (At this point, the facilitator should provide a list of support services ranging from counseling services to designated university personnel responsible for assisting those targeted by bullying.)

Expect the Discussion to be Charged

In addition to providing background and context information, facilitators should anticipate that the conversations following the performance or video may become charged. UAA has an internationally recognized Difficult Dialogues program for engaging campuses in controversial topics and has produced a handbook called *Start Talking* (available free of charge online at www.difficultdialoguesuaa.org or for purchase from your favorite bookseller). Facilitators can borrow from the classroom techniques described in *Start Talking* and adapt them for faculty discussions on bullying. Helpful techniques include:

Code of conduct (p. 12). Invite audience members to establish their own expectations for how they will respectfully interact with one another during the discussion.

Quick/reflective writing (p. 28). Invite audience members to take a few minutes to respond in writing before engaging with the question(s) in open discussion. You can provide a prompt—such as one of the Discussion Questions included in this chapter—or simply ask people to reflect on their responses to the performance or video.

Encircled circle (p. 84). Invite your audience to break into small groups and discuss the deliberately open-ended question, "What is at stake here?" Then have the large group come back together and invite one or two people from each small group to form a small inner circle, with the remaining participants arrayed in a larger circle around them. Each member of the inner circle is invited to sum up the issues and themes discussed in their small group while those in the outer circle listen quietly. You can also invite anyone from the larger group to occupy the inner circle and share their own responses to the question. When they are finished, they can exit the inner circle and someone else from the larger group can take their place. Alternatively, you can simply ask people to join the inner circle and speak directly from the heart.

Listening pairs (not covered in *Start Talking*). Divide audience members into groups of two; one member of the pair shares aloud while the other listens attentively without interruption. After a set amount of time (for example, two minutes), the second person speaks and the first person listens for the same amount of time. You can employ the listening pairs once (for example, immediately after viewing the performance) or multiple times to better ensure that the discussion remains civil and inclusive.

This technique has many benefits for group discussions, including:
- allowing shy people (or people who don't like to compete for airspace in large groups) to voice their thoughts in a safer setting before speaking in the larger group;
- permitting people to vent some of their more charged emotional reactions to the material before engaging in discussion;
- giving everyone in the room a chance to be heard;
- allowing people time to process new information they've encountered;
- modeling the practice of giving everyone equal time to speak, as opposed to allowing some speakers to dominate; and
- giving the discussion leader a few minutes to reflect on where things need to go next.

Be Prepared for Special Cases

We recommend that discussion facilitators recognize two special cases and share the following response strategies:

Violence
Any threat of violence to self or others demands a specialized response. Identify the individuals or units at your university who are responsible for providing that response and keep their phone numbers handy. Examples include campus police, human resources personnel, a designated dean or director, or a care team if one exists. Know when to call 911. It might be helpful to invite professionals to address department meetings, detailing the steps that should be taken when there are concerns about violence. We strongly suggest you take proactive steps to identify these strategies and resources before you need them.

Severe emotional distress
The Americans with Disabilities Act (ADA) protects individuals in the workplace who are suffering from trauma or from severe emotional and mental challenges. It is important to avoid diagnosing or otherwise labeling an individual's behavior and to follow your institutions protocols for ADA compliance. Check with your human resources department or other designated authority for specific steps that will help you honor both the law and the individual(s) involved. We also recommend reading "Working Effectively with Psychologically Impaired Faculty" by Oxenford and Kuhlenschmidt (2011).

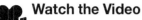

Watch the Video
http://www.difficultdialoguesuaa.org/toxicfriday/
Username: toxicfriday
Password: t0xiC*!#

Discussion Questions

To help launch productive discussions, we've developed a series of questions tied to the live or video performance of *Toxic Friday*. We suggest that you screen the entire performance and talk-back session, then view individual scenes one at a time and invite your audience to engage with one or more of the following questions.

Scene 1 Rachel's office

Toxic Friday portrays several subtle and active toxic behaviors. In real life, much bullying is covert and hard to identify, such as hostile assignment of coursework or critical peer or tenure reviews. It may even involve inaction rather than action (e.g., failure to share information or to include someone in important discussions or social events, delaying important decisions, etc.). What kinds of toxic behaviors have you experienced or heard of others experiencing?

How would you define toxic behavior in a department? In the workplace?

When does incivility rise to the level of bullying? See sample definitions, page 16.

Consider Simon's behavior, both verbal and nonverbal (body language, patterns of eye contact, use of space, etc.). Identify potentially problematic dimensions of his behavior.

Consider Rachel's responses, both verbal and nonverbal. Identify other possible responses she could make.

What could you do if a colleague refused to leave your office? Made these kinds of remarks?

What could you do if a colleague told you these things had happened to him or her?

Scene 2 Department meeting

As faculty gather for the meeting…

We learn that Simon has a history of sending critical email messages about individuals and copying or blind-copying others in the department. What do you think should be done about such behavior? By whom?

As Carol confronts Simon in Rachel's office…

Intimidated, Rachel left Simon in her office when she headed for the department meeting. What other choices might she have had? What risks might she have faced if she'd taken another path?

Charles acknowledges that Simon has targeted others in the past. He also suggests Emily will eventually become a target. Do other members of the department bear responsibility or culpability if, knowing the problem exists, they fail to act?

What might explain Charles's seeming indifference to the plight of his more junior colleagues?

Consider how this situation could be handled by other faculty members within the department. By the chair? By the dean? By others?

What if these parties have taken action, but the problem has not been sufficiently addressed at higher levels within the institution?

At the meeting…

Simon makes several highly inappropriate comments, and no one intervenes. What actions might the chair or other faculty members take to effectively prevent or intervene in such behavior?

Carol brought *Robert's Rules of Order* as a way to promote civil behavior during the meeting. What other tools could the department use to help ensure civil discussions?

If you were to craft a code of conduct for your own department, what would be included? How might it be enforced?

What is the chair's role in intervening in toxic behavior in the department? Do chairs at your university have authority to act or does your institution have a leader-among-peers model? What are the advantages and disadvantages of these models with respect to toxic behavior in departments?

If senior faculty know there is a toxic dynamic within a department, is it right to charge a junior faculty member with a leadership role (like serving as chair)?

After the meeting...

Does Simon's comment that "it's a good thing you have tenure!" raise questions about Carol's responsibility to protect her junior faculty members?

Taken together, do Simon's behaviors rise to the level of bullying? Why or why not?

Scene 3 In the hallway

Charles apologizes to Rachel, referring to Simon's behavior as a "hazing program." Is it appropriate to joke about what is happening?

Charles tells Rachel he supports her and offers to talk further; however, he also minimizes her distress. He tells her to "suck it up," and implies that she is overreacting. Is she?

Scene 4 Silent scene

Rachel has turned to the chair for support and talks with her at great length, venting her distress and potentially exhausting the chair. What are some of the individual, departmental, and institutional costs associated with toxic behavior?

What resources should be made available to targets of toxic behavior?

Scene 5 Carol's office

Carol provides additional confirmation that Simon's behavior has been going on for some time. Does this long history change the institution's responsibility to act?

What steps would you take at your institution when confronting toxic behavior? What policies, procedures, offices, or entities exist to address these situations?

Carol turned to the dean, her human resources office, and the union for support, but says that without a physical threat she could not get traction with her complaint. What does it take to get intervention or support from the proper sources at your institution?

Carol tells Emily she should talk with Dean Stone, but refuses to go with her. Nonetheless, she says, "You have my support." Why do you think Carol is unwilling to accompany Emily?

Why do you think Emily—a second year assistant professor—is willing to risk her job, and possibly her academic career, to file a complaint against Simon?

Scene 6   Dean Stone's office

As the scene opens, it becomes clear that Simon has already gone to the dean. Adult bullies are often charming and endearing to those above them in the power structure while targeting those with equal or less power. Does Simon's behavior fall into this category?

What should a dean or other higher official in an institution do to avoid being manipulated by a bully?

Does the dean need to create and maintain better boundaries to preserve an independent perspective?

Dean Stone says it takes two parties to be involved in a conflict. Is this always true?

Dean Stone tells two junior faculty members that she is confident the faculty within the department can work this issue out on their own. What do you think might happen if two junior faculty members initiated a conversation about this issue at the department level? How might the situation change if those junior faculty members did or did not belong to societally marginalized groups?

Dean Stone asked Carol, the chair, if there was anything else she wanted to talk about. Why do you think Carol did not use this opening to discuss the problems in her department? Should Dean Stone have raised the issue directly? Why do you think she didn't?

General Questions

Many other questions can be useful for deepening your exploration of these and closely related issues.

Gender, Race, Culture
Imagine *Toxic Friday* with different faculty in the roles. What if Simon were a junior faculty member? A woman? What if Simon or Rachel were individuals of color or from another social group that suffers from prejudice or discrimination? What if Simon's primary target was male? An international faculty member (like Emily)? What different interpretations would result from casting this piece in different ways?

Disagreements
How are disagreements and difficult dialogues typically resolved in your department? How should they be?

Hiring and Promotion
When making decisions about who to hire in academic departments, what priority should be placed on diversity or collegiality? Should these considerations be part of promotion and tenure decisions? Who should decide?

Academic Freedom
How should free speech, academic freedom, and the rights of faculty to function in a safe department and institution be simultaneously protected?

Training
Do chairs and deans at your institution receive training to help them effectively intervene in toxic departmental dynamics? If so, is the training effective? If not, what more should it include?

Seniority and Rank
In what ways does faculty seniority make a difference in these dynamics? Faculty rank? How does Simon's new position of authority on the promotion and tenure committee affect the dynamics of the situation? How do these issues play out in even wider contexts, e.g., with adjuncts, staff, undergraduate students, or graduate students in the department, other departments?

Nonverbal Dynamics

Consider the nonverbal dynamics in play. How do they influence your interpretation of the issues? How might other nonverbal behaviors change the dynamics?

Next Steps

What are the next steps your institution needs to take to promote a more collegial working environment?

Suggested Activities

Try these first in pairs or small groups, then invite participants to share with the larger group.

- Divide into groups. Pick a scene from *Toxic Friday* and reenact it with a different outcome.

- Craft and share a scene you believe is missing from *Toxic Friday* but could easily be included. You might, for example, add a scene to the end in which faculty members file a formal complaint. How does the human resource office respond?

- Draft a brief code of conduct that could be used in the weekly faculty meetings depicted in *Toxic Friday*. Share your code of conduct with others. Consider taking these back to departments for discussion and possible use.

- Imagine someone from outside your department approaches you with a story of bullying or toxic behavior. What advice would you offer? What resources could you recommend? Can you suggest someone to talk to? Is there an anonymous hotline to which you might report the situation? What steps might you take to support your colleague?

3

Staging Toxic Friday On Your Campus

Tips for Directors

By Suzanne Burgoyne

Directing an interactive theater event requires the same skills as directing plays for the traditional theater, plus a clear understanding of the distinct conventions and purposes of the interactive form. Successful directors know how to shape performances to suit the particular purposes of this form.

Like its more traditional cousin, interactive theater includes a scripted performance before a live audience. The difference comes with two additional features: *talk-back sessions* and *interventions*. The talk-back session is a mix of scripted material and improvisation in which actors remain in character after the performance to answer questions from the audience. For interventions, the actors begin to perform the script again, but this time audience members are invited to become spect-actors. They can call out "Stop!" whenever they wish and come onstage to try out their own ideas and solutions.

To prepare for these interactive sessions, the director works closely with the actors to create detailed character biographies and to rehearse with them possible questions, answers, and intervention scenarios. This preparation helps the actors respond spontaneously and consistently to questions about their characters' motivations, concerns, perceptions, histories, and relationships with other characters in the scene.

> Dr. Suzanne Burgoyne is Curators' Distinguished Teaching Professor of Theatre and Director of the Center for Applied Theatre and Drama Research at the University of Missouri. She serves on the Board of the Difficult Dialogues National Resource Center and as Producing Director of the Interactive Theatre Troupe (Mizzou ITT), a performance group that specializes in working with faculty, staff, and students on issues of power and privilege—in the classroom and beyond.

Scripting and Casting Concerns

In ideal circumstances, interactive theater actors are paid professionals who can devote sufficient time to the production to prepare for the improvisational and interactive requirements of the performance. The Interactive Theatre Troupe (Mizzou ITT) has ongoing base funding to hire student and professional actors to perform in its productions. UAA secured one-time support for this purpose from a faculty union and the Provost's office.

Unfortunately, even with the luxury of funding, directors don't usually have an unlimited supply of actors to work with. Available acting talent varies widely, and scheduling issues reduce the pool even further. It can be tempting to cast someone simply because in real life he or she occupies the role being portrayed. However, it is not generally a good idea to cast a faculty member to play a faculty member unless he or she is also a seasoned actor.

Specific casting decisions can dramatically change the nature of the dynamics portrayed. In *Toxic Friday*, a middle-aged white male bullies a middle-aged white female. Both the chair and the dean are female, one faculty member is foreign born, and another (the chair) is "of color." The dynamics would look very different (and prompt other kinds of discussions) with different actor demographics, such as if the bully was younger, female, of color, or untenured, and the bully's target much older or younger, male, of color, or tenured.

The *Toxic Friday* producers wanted a cast that included both genders, multiple ethnicities and at least one character who is foreign born. The director cast the best available actors and then had them workshop the script by playing various roles. Final casting decisions incorporated both the capacities of the actors and an awareness of the kinds of bullying dynamics the producers hoped to portray. Other directors working with different variables might cast actors with entirely different characteristics, resulting in a very different set of bullying dynamics. Character names, genders, ethnicities, and many other characteristics can be changed as appropriate.

Developing Character Biographies and Talking Points

In all forms of scripted theater, actors create backstories for the roles they are preparing to play. These backstories are particularly important for interactive performances. Talk-back sessions and interventions require the actors to have a firm grasp on the context in which they are operating and on their characters' specific attitudes, beliefs, and background within that context. The actors won't know the answer to every question the audience may throw at them, but they should know their characters well enough that they can answer spontaneously, in character, from a consistent and believable point of view.

In *Toxic Friday*, it was particularly important that the actors understand the higher education setting. Since few of the available actors had this personal experience, the director spent a significant amount of preparation time getting them up to speed on how a university system works, how their characters fit into that system, and what it means to be faculty member in this situation.

With the context as background, the actor then analyzes the character as portrayed in the script. Who is this person? Where did he come from? What does she want? What values, beliefs, and assumptions does he or she reveal? From here the director and actors develop a set of talking points, pieces of important background information meant to be revealed during the talk-back session in order for the audience to understand more clearly what they just witnessed. One of our Mizzou ITT scripts has a character named Ken who in one scene becomes extremely upset when another character half-teasingly implies that he might be gay. To understand Ken's reaction, the audience needs to learn that this is not an isolated incident: Ken has been mocked and bullied all his life by people assuming he was gay.

Talking points can become nearly as fixed as the script. They remain the same no matter which actor is playing the role. With a script already in the repertoire, the major talking points may be written into a background information sheet given to each new actor playing a role in that play.

Character biographies, on the other hand, need to be created by each individual actor. Actors often use personal analogies to relate to the characters they portray; drawing upon things they know makes it easier to improvise. For instance, an actor from Chicago may decide that his character grew up in Chicago (if such a choice would be appropriate); the actor can then draw upon his knowledge of Chicago when improvising. In the script example above, the actor who plays Ken may choose to play him as straight, as gay but in the closet, or as gay but in denial—whichever choice works best for that actor. The talking point is that Ken has been accused of being gay throughout his life and has been deeply hurt by assumptions people have made about his sexual identity.

At Mizzou ITT, we ask actors to write out a character biography for each role and give it to the director, who may suggest other choices as well. For example, it helps audiences to engage and empathize with a character when he or she tells a meaningful, personal story in the talk-back session. In one of our scripts, a Muslim character is looked upon with suspicion by another character who fears the Muslim is a terrorist. A Muslim actor who played the Muslim role in that script a few years after 9/11 told us of coming home on that fateful day to find her father watching television and crying. We incorporated that story into the actor's character biography.

Rehearsals

Any rehearsal for an ITT event includes a rehearsal of the talk-back session as well as the scripted performance. To prepare the actors for audience questioning, the director and other actors ask sample questions that prompt the actor to use the information created in his or her character biography in response. Together, the director and actors decide which type of questions will be answered in *timed-in mode* (with all the other characters listening) and which the character would want to answer in *timed-out mode* (privately, as if none of the other characters can hear the response). When characters answer questions publicly, they may argue with each other; the talk-back rehearsal allows actors to discover and practice potential interactions.

Interventions

Although one never knows what a spect-actor may do onstage, directors may also find it helpful to rehearse an intervention or two. The facilitator should warn the spect-actors that neither magic nor mayhem is allowed in an intervention. The solution can't be "Abracadabra! Now you all love each other!" Nor are spect-actors allowed to beat up on actors. With those two exceptions, the actors need to be prepared to respond in character to whatever the spect-actor may do.

There is an important difference between ordinary improvisation and how an ITT actor improvises during an intervention. Ordinarily, an actor will pursue his character's objective no matter what. In interactive theater, however, the actor has to keep in mind the educational goal of the performance. The character should not give in too easily but neither should he crush the spect-actor.

> **Exercise:**
> **How Hard to Push**
>
> Each person in the group finds a partner. The partners stand face to face with about two feet separating them. Partners should then place their palms together and push against each other, trying to determine how hard they can push without "winning." The goal is not to see who is stronger but to push against the other person just as much as she pushes against you. Once the partners have gotten the hang of this activity, variations can be employed such as, "see how hard you can push without the audience noticing" and "see how lightly you can push without losing tension."

We often use an exercise to give the actors practice in the kind of response an intervention calls for. This exercise serves as a physical metaphor for how actors need to work with spect-actors. It takes courage for a spect-actor to come onstage, and the actors should not punish him for taking a risk. Interventions should not be easy, but they should not be impossible. Similarly, character feedback to a spect-actor works best when it's constructive (though, of course, given in character). It may help actors meet the challenge of remaining true to their character—and at the same time not "pushing" too hard—for each actor to think about what her character would need in order to respond more positively to the situation explored in the scene.

Outcomes and Happy Endings

Interactive theater can provide significant learning experiences for the actors as well as for the audiences. The problems portrayed are complex and difficult to solve, and actors are thrilled when an audience member offers a solution that works. Some performances end happily with an intervention that can be applied to real life and an approach in which everybody learns something along the way. In the best cases, everybody wins.

A former student who had been active in Mizzou ITT was recently interviewed for an article in our alumni magazine. "It's amazing what we did to audiences," he said. "I saw people come in, ask questions, and have light bulbs go off. That's incredible when you're talking about things like race, gender, or sexuality—to have these conversations and not have to agree, to even say things that might sound controversial. When it happens and people listen, it changes people. It's powerful. Some days I wonder, 'Why am I not devoting my life to this?' This is the kind of thing that can change the world."[1]

---

1 Whit Loy, quoted in Erik Potter, "Acting Outside the Box," *Mizzou Magazine* (Winter 2015).

The Script

Interactive scripts are designed to be flexible. In early drafts, characters are written for actors of either gender, with generic names such as "DR. A" or dual names such as "SIMON/SIMONE." These conventions keep the script open for as long as possible during the development period and give directors the greatest amount of flexibility in casting new productions. Once a script is finalized for a particular repertory company or performance, details are changed to match the characteristics and preferences of the chosen actors.

The script that follows is our final stage draft and film production script, reflecting the choices made by the UAA producing, directing, and acting team. It was developed and honed in rehearsal for maximum clarity, precision, and, most importantly, performability. Character names are specified (Simon Albertson, Rachel Nichols, etc.), and the pronouns match these genders.

Groups who wish to stage their own live performances may customize the script in a variety of ways. Details can be changed to accompany different backstories, to support different talking points, or to create different subtexts for discussion. Each change of character name, gender, ethnicity, rank, political persuasion, or other identifier changes the dynamics of the situation and opens the script up to new directions for discussion.

Dr. Andréa J. Onstad is the author of numerous original plays, including "Plane Crash," "Jukebox," and "A Knock on the Door." Her work has been performed in venues throughout the United States and Europe, including the Actors Studio-First Stage in Los Angeles, York and Vineyard Theatres in New York, and the New English American Theatre in Germany. Publications include "Deer Haunting: A Far Side Cartoon" in the *Best American Short Plays 2012-13* and "Teddy '77" in *Elvis Monologues*. She has an MFA from the Iowa Playwrights Workshop and a Ph.D. in Theatre-Writing for Performance from the University of Missouri.

TOXIC FRIDAY

A University of Alaska Anchorage
Center for Advancing Faculty Excellence
Difficult Dialogues Project

Written by
Dr. Andréa J. Onstad

in collaboration with

Dr. Gabrielle Barnett, Dr. Suzanne Burgoyne,
Libby Roderick, and other anonymous consultants,

and

Jane Baird, Joan Cullinane, Vivian Kinnaird,
Tami Lubitsh, John McKay, Todd Sherwood, and
Kelly Lee Williams, actors

CHARACTERS

SIMON ALBERTSON Full Professor and newly appointed chair of the College Promotion and Tenure Committee

CHARLES BAKER Full Professor, nearing retirement

EMILY COHEN Assistant Professor, second year

CAROL DALTON Full Professor and outgoing department chair

RACHEL NICHOLS Assistant Professor, fourth year

DEAN STONE Dean of the College of Liberal Arts and Interdisciplinary Studies

TIME

The present

PLACE

The American Studies Department of a large university

Characters and material are fictitious. Resemblance to any persons, living or dead, is strictly coincidental.

Scene 1

                    (RACHEL's office. RACHEL is on phone, computer)

                              RACHEL
...uh huh...uh huh...I'd love to but...Friday meeting in
a few...yeah...I dread it...I'm stressed out and my blood
pressure...Oh! He just sent me another email!... criticizing
my research!...must've read my Alcotts article in American
Quarterly...yeah...right...he hasn't published anything
in years...could be why he keeps picking on me...but...
tenure...gotta be cautious...

                    (SIMON appears at RACHEL's door)

                         RACHEL (Cont'd)
                    (Whispering)
...oh god, speak of the devil...he's at my door. Gotta go.
Text you later. Bye.
                    (To SIMON)
Simon?!

                              SIMON
                    (Enters without waiting for invitation,
                    advancing close—too close)
I hope I'm not intruding, Rachel, but after I sent my last
email I had another thought. You should make me co-author
of your next article. What do you think? Tenure file's due
soon...

                              RACHEL
I think—

                              SIMON
                    (Straining to look at computer screen)
New research? I hope it's more substantive than the last.

                              RACHEL
                    (Closing computer)
I think we're going to be late.

                    (RACHEL rises, begins to move towards door)

                    SIMON
          (Rising as if to follow, snoops instead; sees
          paper on RACHEL's desk)
Did you hear I'm now Chair of the College Promotion and
Tenure Committee?

                    RACHEL
          (At door)
No, I didn't...

                    SIMON
          (Picks up paper, starts reading)
Hmmm. Reviewer comments...These are embarrassing!

          (RACHEL hesitates at door)

                    RACHEL
I...We...really need to leave...

                    SIMON
          (Reading)
You need help with this. If you really wanted tenure you'd
ask me....

                    RACHEL
But I...need to lock up...would you mind...?
          (Indicates leaving)

                    SIMON
          (Reading)
I'll lock up.

                    RACHEL
          (Hesitates, checks time, sighs)
But...

                    SIMON
          (Reading)
Go ahead. I said I'll lock up.

          (RACHEL checks time again, sighs, exits)

Scene 2

(Conference room. CHARLES and EMILY, relaxed, chitchatting)

CHARLES
Have you been to the Crusty Ram yet?

EMILY
No, I haven't.

CHARLES
It's a must. And hey, it's Friday. You could go this weekend.

EMILY
I might do that. After I finish grading. Thanks for the suggestion. Aren't you going on sabbatical soon?

CHARLES
Couldn't come soon enough!

EMILY
You must be so excited.

CHARLES
I am. San Francisco Bay Area, here I come! Home of three major Steinbeck collections!

(RACHEL enters, sits, dejected; puts cell phone where she can see it)

EMILY
Are you okay?

CHARLES
Let me guess. The email?

RACHEL
How did you—?

CHARLES
I was bcc'd.

                              EMILY
So was I.

                             RACHEL
Isn't there any privacy around here?

                            CHARLES
We've all been through it.

                              EMILY
I haven't.

                            CHARLES
You will.

                             RACHEL
                    (To CHARLES)
What did you do?

                            CHARLES
Nothing. Shook it off. Like water on a—

                             RACHEL
                    (Cutting off CHARLES)
It's different now...he's—

                    (Offstage commotion begins—SIMON and CAROL;
                    RACHEL, CHARLES, EMILY listen)

                             CAROL
                    (Offstage)
What are you doing in Rachel's office?

                              SIMON
                    (Offstage)
Good afternoon to you, too, Dr. Dalton.

                             CAROL
                    (Offstage, louder)
I said, what are you doing in Rachel's office??!!

                    SIMON
               (Offstage, loud)
She left in a tizzy. She needs help with this. I offered,
she....

                    CAROL
               (Offstage, cutting off, louder)
She what? Said you could trespass?! I should report you.
               (Storms off; footsteps audible)

                    SIMON
               (Offstage, calling after, louder)
Knock yourself out. I was just leaving anyway.
               (Slams office door)

                    RACHEL
Oh my head.

               (RACHEL reaches for a pill, takes it)

                    CAROL
               (Offstage, walking away, calling back)
And stop sending her those emails.

                    SIMON
               (Offstage, shouting after)
Some chairs encourage mentoring.

                    EMILY
Like five-year olds!

                    CHARLES
               (To RACHEL)
It'll be okay.

                    EMILY
               (To RACHEL)
Did you really leave your office with him in it?

                    RACHEL
Yes. I did. He wouldn't leave. I felt threatened. And
like I started to say, he's now—

                        EMILY
              (Cutting RACHEL off)
Well I would never—

                        CHARLES
              (Cutting EMILY off; to RACHEL)
He's irritating, yes, but harmless.

              (CAROL storms in, angry, carrying Roberts Rules
              of Order; goes to head of table; does not sit;
              busies herself with meeting preparations.

              SIMON follows right behind; goes to opposite end
              of table from CAROL, sits, grins.

              CHARLES, EMILY, RACHEL visibly shift closer
              together, away from SIMON)

                        SIMON
Happy Friday everyone. Why the sad faces?

                        CAROL
              (To SIMON)
Why can't we just get along.

                        SIMON
              (To CAROL)
You're too sensitive.

              (CAROL slams book on table.

              CHARLES, EMILY, RACHEL jump)

                        CHARLES
              (To CAROL)
Robert's Rules of Order...?!

                    CAROL
          (Glaring at SIMON; to CHARLES)
A reminder to keep our meetings civil.
          (Looking around)
Looks like we're all here. Let's get started.
          (Goes to whiteboard if available)
We've got a big agenda.
          (Writing)
Chair Chair Chair Chair Chair
          (Finishing, turning)
Who's going to be the next chair?
That's our agenda. Our only agenda.

                    EMILY
And my senior seminar proposal.

                    CAROL
What proposal?

                    EMILY
I sent you an email—

                    CAROL
I didn't get it.

                    CHARLES
          (To EMILY)
You're new. It probably went into her junk mail.

                    EMILY
I'm in my second year.

                    SIMON
She doesn't read email. She only sends it.

                    CAROL
Moving on.

                    EMILY
          (To CAROL)
But can we add it?

                    CAROL
Come to my office later. We'll talk.

                    SIMON
          (Smirks)

                    CAROL
Back to the agenda. Chair. Who is willing...

          (Silence.

          CHARLES, tentative, raises hand)

                    CAROL
Why, Charles, I had no idea—

                    CHARLES
          (Cutting CAROL off)
No, no, not me. I'm not going to be around. I need to talk
about my sabb—

          (Objections from EMILY and RACHEL)

                    SIMON
          (Leaning toward EMILY and RACHEL who recoil)
          He means his trip to California.

                    CHARLES
          (Noticing objections)
—but we can save meeting time and do that later.

                    CAROL
That's what I like. Someone who understands the value of
meeting time. Thank you, Charles. Anyone else?

          (Another pause.

          SIMON raises hand)

                    CAROL
          (Surprised)
Simon!

SIMON

Not what you think. I'm way too busy. If you read your
email you would know I am now official Chair of the College
Promotion and Tenure Committee.

          (Stunned silence; RACHEL retreats into cell
          phone, texts)

          SIMON (Cont'd)
And the Provost tapped me to address the Regents next week.

          ALL (except SIMON)
!!!

          (Pause)

          EMILY
Let me be the first to congratulate you, but with all due
respect, this is a different topic.

          SIMON
          (To EMILY)
Oh, recognizing when something's a different topic!
Dr. Cohen, is that how you won the Hells Angels Prize?

          EMILY
!!! Angela Y. Davis Prize!

          SIMON
Same difference.
          (To ALL)
By the way, I've nominated Dr. Cohen to the Diversity
Oversight Committee. Isn't she perfect for it?
          (To EMILY)
You'll need service.

          EMILY
I appreciate your interest in my career, Dr. Albertson, but
we're talking about the next department chair, not committee
nominations.

                         CAROL
                  (To EMILY)
Thank you Emily, but I'm running this meeting. When you
become chair you can run the meetings.
                  (To ALL)
So— all of you— congratulate Simon afterwards— but now, back
to the agenda. Who wants to be chair.

                  (During the above, RACHEL begins texting in
                  earnest.

                  SIMON watches for a bit. Then—)

                         SIMON
                  (Pointing to RACHEL)
Can you believe her?

                  (All attention on RACHEL)

                         CAROL
Focus. Everyone.

                  (RACHEL puts cell phone away, embarrassed;
                  withdraws)

                         SIMON
                  (Smirks)

                         CAROL
                  (To everyone, frustrated)
Look. Nobody wants to be chair. But someone has to or our
department could be in trouble. Sense of duty anyone?

                  (No response)

                         CAROL (Cont'd)
                  (More frustrated)
No? Then what about self-interest? Is there something you
want? Your chances of getting it are better as chair.

                         EMILY
That makes sense.

CAROL

Thank you, Emily. Are you interested?

EMILY

No! No! I'm too new. I'm interested in what you're saying. It makes a lot of sense.

CAROL.

It should. I've been around a long time.

EMILY

Then why not stay chair? Experience—

CAROL

Oh no. I'm done. Look at me. I'm a wreck.

EMILY

I see that.

CAROL
(To RACHEL)
Rachel. You're awfully quiet. Would you—?

RACHEL

No! Oh nonono! I'm— I'm overloaded— courses, committees, getting ready to go up for tenure— I cannot—
(Pause, agitated)
Would you excuse me for a moment?

CAROL

Of course.

(RACHEL exits. RACHEL is heard emotional offstage. A moment)

SIMON

I have a suggestion.

CAROL

Only if it relates to our agenda.

                    SIMON
It does. I move we nominate Rachel chair.

          (A moment. RACHEL enters)

                    CAROL
          (To RACHEL)
Rachel, while you were out of the room, Dr. Albertson
nominated you chair.

                    RACHEL
          (Disarmed)
But— I'm not— tenured.

                    SIMON
It's easy. Anybody can do it.

                    CAROL
I'm going to talk to Dean Stone. Meeting adjourned.

          (RACHEL rushes out, cell phone to ear.

          CHARLES hurries after.

          SIMON moves to leave, lurks near door.

          CAROL is packing up.

          EMILY approaches CAROL)

                    EMILY
          (To CAROL)
So my proposal? I want to do a senior seminar on the
cultural significance of modern pop stars. Did you hear
about that? On NPR? Cutting edge pedagogy...?

                    CAROL
          (Distracted, packing up)
What would the syllabus look like.

                    EMILY
Well, I haven't—

                    CAROL
             (Cutting EMILY off)
Let's see what's going to happen with the department before
making any changes, okay?

                    EMILY
So—?

                    CAROL
Stick with the classics. You're teaching Emerson. I love
Emerson—

                    EMILY
I love him, too, but he's dead and we've got to stay alive.
             (EMILY exits)

             (CAROL attempts to leave.
             SIMON blocks her exit)

                    CAROL
Excuse me.

                    SIMON
Aren't you going to congratulate me?

                    CAROL
What for? Messing with junior faculty?
Let me pass!
             (CAROL pushes past SIMON, exits)

                    SIMON
             (Yelling after)
It's a good thing you have tenure!!!

Scene 3

(Hallway.

RACHEL is talking on her cell phone.

CHARLES hurries to catch up with her)

> RACHEL
> (On cell phone)
> Bad news. I've been nominated chair. And you know me—(I can't say no).

(CHARLES catches up with RACHEL)

> RACHEL (Cont'd)
> —gotta go. Call me.
> (Ends call)

> CHARLES
> Can I talk to you a minute.

> RACHEL
> I'm— expecting a call—

> CHARLES
> I just want to say how sorry I am. And if it's any consolation, we've all been through it. Well, except for Emily, who is getting a taste. We call it "The Dr. Albertson American Studies Faculty Hazing Program." Part of the process.
> (Chuckles)

> RACHEL
> I don't find it funny Charles; I find it terrifying.

> CHARLES
> I understand but I still don't think you should take it—or him—too seriously.

> RACHEL
> I don't know how else to take it. My career is on the line. And so is my health.

                         CHARLES
Look. You'd make a great chair. The tenure thing? Won't
be a problem.

                         RACHEL
You mean I'll be granted tenure in order to be chair?

                         CHARLES
That's not going to happen. But I'm sure Carol will go to
Dean Stone and get the requirement waived. We need a chair.
You're the obvious choice.

                         RACHEL
I better talk to Carol.

                         CHARLES
Sometimes we have to suck it up.

                         RACHEL
And do things we don't want to do? Like not go on
sabbatical and be chair?

                         CHARLES
Oh nonono. I wish I could help but I've worked too hard for
this. Come by my office if you want to talk some more. I'll
be here until the end of the semester, ten more weeks and
three more days! Just know I'm with you, Rachel.

          (CHARLES exits.

          CAROL enters brisk, en route to office from
          meeting, frazzled, distracted, still angry from
          encounter with SIMON.

          RACHEL rushes to catch her)

                         RACHEL
Could I talk to you?

                         CAROL
In my office.

Scene 4

(Silent scene. Several hours pass.

RACHEL unloads her woes on CAROL.

SIMON complains to DEAN STONE about the department.

EMILY and CHARLES go about their normal business)

Scene 5

        (CAROL's office. Several hours later.

        CAROL is exhausted.

        RACHEL has finished unloading; takes a pill)

              RACHEL
        (Indicating pill)
Blood pressure.

              CAROL
Don't worry about it. We all take pills.

              RACHEL
I didn't mean to unload on you. I'm just so overwhelmed.
And most of it sounds so silly—

              CAROL
It's not silly.

              RACHEL
I've thought about reporting it but what would I say?

              CAROL
I started to do that a few years ago—

              RACHEL
Same problem?

              CAROL
Same person.

              RACHEL
!!!

                    CAROL
We started out friends. When I became chair and didn't back
him he— anyway I had nightmares for months. Eventually I
went to the Dean— a different Dean then. He told me to go
to HR. So I went to HR. HR told me to go to the Union. So
I went to the Union. The Union told me to go to HR.

                    RACHEL
So...?

                    CAROL
I didn't. Without a direct physical threat I didn't have a
case. I would either have to leave or learn to swim with the
sharks.

          (A knock at the door)

                    CAROL
Come in.

          (EMILY enters)

                    EMILY
          (Sees RACHEL; to CAROL)
Oh! Excuse me. Am I interrupting?
          (To RACHEL)
I am so so sorry.
          (To CAROL)
Do you have a moment?

                    CAROL
Sure.

                    RACHEL
I was just leaving.

                    EMILY
You don't have to.

                    RACHEL
I've taken up too much of Carol's time already.

                    EMILY
No, stay. It may be relevant. It's about Simon.

                    CAROL
We were just talking about him/her.

                    EMILY
I'm seriously considering filing a complaint.

                    CAROL
If you do, you better have an exit strategy.

                    EMILY
I know— I know— it's a bad career move, but I've worked with
people like him before. I just can't again.

                    CAROL
At least talk to Dean Stone first. Chain of command, you
know.

                    EMILY
Will you come?

                    CAROL
No, but you've got my support.

                    EMILY
Rachel? It can't hurt to talk.

                    RACHEL
There's nothing to lose I suppose.

          (EMILY and RACHEL exit)

Scene 6

(DEAN STONE's office. EMILY and RACHEL arrive just as SIMON is leaving)

SIMON

Ladies— I'm just leaving. She's all yours. Have a wonderful weekend.
(To DEAN STONE, exiting)
See you at the racquetball court Sunday?

DEAN STONE
(Calling after SIMON)
I'll try but no promises. Get that hearing tested— nothing to be ashamed of. And kudos on the P&T!
(To EMILY and RACHEL)
Such dedication. P&T is a timesink, but he said he'll enjoy it. That's Dr. Albertson for you. But please come in. Sit. Sit.

(EMILY and RACHEL enter, sit, stunned)

EMILY	RACHEL
Thank you.	Thank you.

DEAN STONE

What can I do for you ladies?

EMILY

We—

DEAN STONE

Oh but first let me congratulate you Rachel. Dr. Albertson told me about your recent article. It's wonderful to see our faculty publishing in such prestigious journals.

RACHEL

Thank you.

                    DEAN STONE
And I'm thrilled he has agreed to mentor you. Your next
article should sail right through the review process with
him on board as co-author.

                    RACHEL
!!!

                    DEAN STONE
But please forgive me. I digress. What can I do for you?

                    EMILY
We're here...to...talk about...Simon...

                    DEAN STONE
Yes?

                    EMILY
Well...uh...Simon is...a very impressive researcher and
I'm sure he'll work hard on the P&T Committee, but...uh...
...he's rude...

                    RACHEL
...insulting...

                    EMILY
...intimidating...

                    RACHEL
...threatening...

          (Long silence)

                    DEAN STONE
That's hard to believe. Dr. Albertson mentioned stress in
your department but that's not unusual in a group of bright,
competitive individuals with strong personalities. You must
be misinterpreting his behavior—

                    EMILY
--No, no we are not misinterpreting. Simon is a bully.
Rachel is traumatized from his "mentoring" emails, I have
been harassed and intimidated, Carol has been yelled at—

                    DEAN STONE

--And Carol has never yelled?

                     EMILY

Well...

                    DEAN STONE

It takes two, Dr.—?

                     EMILY

Cohen. Our department meetings are fine until he shows up.
"Toxic Fridays"— that's what Rachel calls them, don't you
Rachel?

                     RACHEL

Worst of all, he nominated me for department chair.

                    DEAN STONE

Quite a compliment, isn't it?

                     RACHEL

Not if you don't—

                     EMILY

--He nominated me for the Diversity Oversight Committee.

                    DEAN STONE

Seems appropriate. But you object?

                     EMILY

It's insulting. The implied tokenism—

                    DEAN STONE

--I think you're overreacting.

                     EMILY

He gets right up in our faces—

                     RACHEL

—close. Like this—
          (Demonstrates)

                    DEAN STONE
He did mention he has a hearing problem and is embarrassed
about it. He's going to get it checked.

                     RACHEL
He wouldn't leave my office today.

                    DEAN STONE
I'm sure he had a reason. If you're having a problem with
Dr. Albertson why don't you talk to him? Or have your chair
do it.

                     EMILY
She's tried. They yell—

                     RACHEL
--We're all so stressed out—

                    DEAN STONE
--I've heard all about it from Dr. Albertson. There's
always more than one side you know. But for the sake of
argument let's say Dr. Albertson has played some part. To
make a case you must have proof— documentation. Do you have
that?

                     EMILY
Well—

                     RACHEL
I could print out all those emails—

                     EMILY
We could write up everything that happened today.

                     RACHEL
And yesterday.

                     EMILY
And last week.

                    DEAN STONE
Have you spoken to HR or the Union?

                         EMILY
No. Carol suggested we come to you first.

                      DEAN STONE
That was wise. Once a formal complaint is filed there is
no going back. Both sides are investigated. Results are
rarely satisfactory for either. My advice? Live with it.
Or, take a deep breath and talk to him.

                         EMILY
Can't you talk to him?

                      DEAN STONE
I did. I didn't see any sign of the person you described.

                         EMILY
So— you won't help—

                      DEAN STONE
I don't see that you have a problem you can't solve
yourselves. Go to HR if you want but you will need more to
report than occasional obnoxious behavior. If that were the
criteria for dismissal, many of our department offices would
be empty!
                  (Chuckles)

                         EMILY
The empty office in our department is likely to be mine.

                      DEAN STONE
               (Laughs)
Dr. Albertson was right. There are strong personalities
in your department. I'm sure you can work this out among
yourselves. But I'm glad you came to talk with me. It's
good to get these concerns out in the open. And I will have
a word with him about being more sensitive to the stress
level in your department.

                  (RACHEL has been sitting silent. She looks at
                  her cell phone)

                    RACHEL
Please excuse me.

                    EMILY
Another email.

                    RACHEL
Yeah.
I need to go. Thanks.
          (Exits)

                    EMILY
I need to go, too. I have a class. Thank you for the
advice.

                    DEAN STONE
You're very welcome.

          (EMILY exits.

          After a moment, CAROL pokes her head into DEAN
          STONE's office)

                    CAROL
Do you have a minute? I have a quick question.

                    DEAN STONE
I have a quick minute.

                    CAROL
          (Entering, sitting)
My term as chair is ending and no one else can do it.
They're either too busy, going on sabbatical, too new, or
too burned out—that's me. In our department meeting today,
Simon nominated Rachel chair. And though Rachel is going
up for tenure soon, she is not tenured right now. We don't
want to jeopardize our department over a technicality.
Could you waive the tenure requirement so Rachel could be
our next chair?

DEAN STONE

I'm sure that won't be a problem. Since Dr. Albertson
nominated Rachel and it sounds as if everyone agrees, I have
complete faith in her abilities. Is there anything else?

CAROL

No. That's it. Thanks for your time.
          (Starts to leave)

DEAN STONE

You're welcome.
Do you play racquetball?

—END—

Backstories and Talking Points

The director and actors employed by UAA worked together to develop backstories and talking points for each character and to rehearse possible talk-back session questions and answers. The actors went in to each talk-back session with a range of possibilities for making the key points. Each event was unique, of course, and the actors were rarely able to get all of their prepared points into the discussion. But the extensive preparation allowed them to be as ready as possible to respond in ways that would help the audience recognize and understand the complex factors that underlie virtually every line in the script.

The following details are neither definitive nor fixed, and some characters are fleshed out more than others. We have compiled these notes to serve as models you can use to develop backstories and talking points that fit your own unique situations and purposes. Feel free to use or adapt these for your own performances or to develop new ones in collaboration with your own actors and directors.

The American Studies department
University of North Carigan

Note: We created a fictional university and department in order to provide a bit of distance for audience members. Our university has no such department or major.

Department Backstory
The American Studies department was formed by Professor Laura Feldspar (now retired) and Professor Charles Baker (soon to retire). Previously, American Studies had been only a minor, with courses cross-listed from English, History, Philosophy, Theater, and Political Science. They hired young go-getter Simon Albertson as the program's first full-time faculty member, to teach Intro to American Studies (a new course) and a senior seminar.

Early on, there were lots of hardball politics on behalf of the new American Studies major, in which Albertson was a key player. He got Carol Dalton hired as the second dedicated American Studies faculty and helped get Feldspar and Baker out of English, where they were frustrated, and into American Studies full time.

As the first hires, Carol Dalton and Simon Albertson were allies in the beginning. Once Albertson was tenured, he helped fast-track Dalton through the tenure process. Later, however, they fell out about vision for the program. Albertson wanted to follow a public policy/Harvard Kennedy School model, and the other three wanted to emphasize arts and letters. Albertson pushed hard for designating a new fifth position as public policy or international relations, but Dalton supported the other direction (that's where the "you refused to back me" comment comes from). Feldspar and the others made sure it was written with a popular culture and theater emphasis instead.

During this time, Albertson turned on Feldspar as public enemy #1. Although ultimately she prevailed, the battle drained her, and she retired early six years ago. Feldspar's vacated position, which was shaped by her specialization in American Women's Studies, is currently occupied by Rachel Nichols.

The original person hired to fill the contentious fifth position was Dr. Leon Kelly, a specialist in African American Theater, American Popular Entertainment (1700-the present), and The American Comedic Voice. He vacated the position three years ago, at the associate level, in the middle of a term as chair. Ostensibly, Kelly got a better offer. In reality he left to get away from the department dysfunction: he'd been through the Feldspar retirement and the Nichols search, and he didn't want to go up for full professor in this environment

Kelly was the only associate professor in the department; after he left, his position was filled by Emily Cohen. Carol Dalton stepped back into the chair position for a second term.

Simon Albertson
Professor

Backstory Notes
Simon exhibited tremendous promise in graduate school, but that great start has essentially gone nowhere; he has not realized his full intellectual potential in the years since. He chose American Studies at least partly to be a big fish in a small pond, and now he wonders if that was the best idea. Perhaps he should have chosen a more respected specialty or a different path that might have led him to Harvard's Kennedy School, Johns Hopkins, or some other university that is better placed than his current one.

He has ended up isolated both intellectually and professionally. All the others in his department have some sort of minority or anti-establishment interest, even Charles Baker (the other white man), who is an expert on the blue collar working man perspective of John Steinbeck. He blames department politics and the direction of American Studies in general for blocking the success and respect he feels he deserves.

Talking Points

- He's a charmer and a flirt, openly flirting with the audience every chance he gets.
- He's a high functioning person with a deep disorder. He doesn't see himself as a bully; he thinks other people are the source of the problem. "Let me tell you about this department. It's like a psychiatrist's dream come true. Emily is a typical feminist Women's Studies (starts to say 'bitch' but catches himself) person who thinks because I'm a successful white male I'm relying on patriarchal privilege. Charles may have a Borderline Personality Disorder: he treats you like a god one minute and like a worm the next. Rachel edges toward nymphomania, and Carol is paranoid."
- He blames others for his long intellectual dry spell. "Maybe I should have taken a different job at a better university. I went for program building over personal achievement. My own research was never respected by my colleagues. They just used me to get the program launched."

Sample Talk-back Q and A's

What made you come to North Carigan? "I love the outdoors."

Do you have a family? In timed-in mode, the answer is, "none of your business." In timed-out mode, he might admit to a bitter divorce: "She ran off with some other guy, or maybe it was a woman, I don't know."

How do you see your relationship with Rachel? In timed-in mode, he might say that he's just trying to help her and the department (even though the department screwed him over). In timed-out mode, he might say, "Well, she came on to me, and I'm just trying to put the relationship back on professional footing. That's why I offered to mentor her."

Charles Baker
Professor

Character Biography

Education: Ph.D. comparative Literature (Linguistics), Stanford University; B.A. in Theater, emphasis on acting and playwriting, Stanislaus State University, California.

Research Interests: Mark Twain's letters and short stories, John Steinbeck's collected works, Jack London's biographies and related works.

Grants: NEA $30,000

Publications (Fiction, Non Fiction, Journalism & Poetry): The South Dakota Review, Over the Transom, MungBeing, Dan River Anthology, Explorations, North Woods Journal, cirque, Driftwood.

Charles was born in Montana, the youngest of seven. His father, a rancher, was a World War II veteran, U.S. Navy, who came home in one piece and became a lifelong Democrat. In 1949, much of the bottom fell out of ranching in Montana. Charles was only eleven years old at the time, but each night after working in the hay fields or grazing cattle, he milked cows at a neighbor's farm to help with family expenses. Charles's father eventually died of alcoholism, and the family sold the ranch and split up. Charles and his mother went to live with an older brother, an accountant who lived in California. This is where Charles attended high school and college.

In high school, Charles encountered many bullies, who made lots of verbal threats and, unlike in Montana, came at him with a gang rather than one-on-one. Charles quickly learned that it was better to take the intimidation and not start swinging when the odds were against him. He learned to let it run "like water off of a duck's back," but often suffered from being branded a coward for not fighting back. He took these lessons with him for the rest of his life. When he became a college professor, he retreated into his books and writing and tried to avoid all conflicts.

Talking Points

- He is on his way out and just doesn't care anymore. "I'm getting older now. I've worked all my life, loved what I've done. I'm not going out as happy as I thought I would be, but some battles just aren't worth fighting."
- He would like to have been a leader but just didn't know how. "Great leaders need to command both fear and respect. I've never been respected enough to get anywhere."
- He is articulate and good at both analysis and analogy. "A university is like a large urban area; departments are like rural areas or small towns. There's very little accountability in the city, you only help those who are close to you. But in small towns, everyone knows everything about you. You can't be anonymous, and you can't move on. You have to get along. City people bring certain attitudes with them, and they try to impose those attitudes on the smaller scale."
- He sees the world through the lens of literature. "It's just like Cannery Row. First it was a fishing village, and now it's a center of tourism. Whenever you have people with different agendas living side by side, you know there are going to be conflicts."

Sample Talk-back Q and A's

What is your definition of bullying? "A bully is someone who acts without thinking of anyone else, who lives in a culture of 'I' not 'we.' Think of it like coaching basketball. In a culture of 'I,' city kids usually need to be reminded to pass the ball more often. In a culture of 'we,' like we see in many rural towns and villages, the players will often pass the ball too much. They are more concerned that everyone has their turn."

Why don't you give up or postpone your sabbatical? "No. I've done my time."

Why don't you do something about Simon? In timed-in mode, he might take the educator's high road: "I don't like politics. I just want to get back to the classroom." In timed-out mode, he might reveal some of his background: "Back where I was raised, we didn't put up with this tomfoolery. We took them out back of the woodshed. That's how we solved our problems. But here, violence is not an option, so we're stuck."

Emily Cohen
Assistant Professor

Backstory Notes
Emily is a theater scholar who won the Angela Y. Davis prize for working with underserved and at-risk youth populations in Chicago and in Cape Town, South Africa. Her work is notable for performing a kind of public service that bridges community engagement and scholarship.

Talking Points
- Having experienced bullying before, she has researched it and is something of an expert on the issue. "Bullies think their behavior is rational: a reasonable response to what's happening. They tend to repeat these behaviors because they get reinforced for them. They are clever at cultivating new people, sucking them in and then zinging them later, using whatever information they gleaned, twisting and turning it to suit their purposes."
- She sees bullying from a feminist perspective. "The men who have bullied me did it because they don't like to see a woman appear to be smarter or more productive than they are. Women in leadership positions are treated very differently from men. Strong accomplished women are often perceived as threatening. Ultimately, it's about power, but not always hierarchical power. Sometimes it's socio-cultural power."
- She blames the administration for allowing bullying to continue. "I think the administration's failure to act is one of the biggest things that contributes to ongoing bullying incidents. I know dealing with personnel issues is not something they enjoy doing, but it's their job."

Sample Talk-back Q and A's
How do you see Simon's behavior? "He doesn't even know he's a bully. Some people act like this because they want to feel better about themselves. They feel unimportant, and this is a way to feel more important and powerful."

Why do people go along with a bully? "Some people want so badly to be part of the group that when they see bullying behavior they do a rough calculation: shall I risk becoming an outsider by standing up for the victim or can I solidify my own place in the group by turning on the victim too?"

How seriously are you thinking about leaving? In timed-out mode, she might tell a story about a bullying manager at a previous job where things were so bad that she had a breakdown and needed therapy to recover.

Carol Dalton
Professor, Department Chair

Backstory Notes
Carol was the second full-time faculty member to be hired for this department, so she has seen it all. At first, she and Simon were allies, and he helped fast-track her through the tenure process. They fell out over the next position to be hired, however, and have had a rocky relationship ever since. She is currently serving her second rotation as department chair, after stepping in to fill the vacuum left by the sudden departure of Leon Kelly.

Talking Points
- She understands the high cost of bullying in her department. "Bullying costs departments millions of dollars nationally, and it makes people emotionally miserable and physically sick."
- She has a theory for why it continues. "With the way our chairs rotate every couple of years, people don't want to mess with someone who may soon be in a position to retaliate. You know you won't be chair forever, and if the next person is somebody you've angered, then you can expect payback."
- She has received virtually no support from the administration. "When I first became chair, they told me, 'Oh, a chair doesn't really do that much. You'll be fine.' Hah! I asked for a handbook and they told me the handbook was over thirty years old and so dated that no one looks at it anymore. I don't know the rules because there are no rules. There's just nothing written down."

Sample Talk-back Q and A's
Why are there no associate professors in your department? In timed-out mode, she could tell the backstory of the department. "The department has been in turmoil almost from the beginning. First there was the clash over the fifth position, then over Feldspar's retirement. Our only associate professor left three years ago, fed up with all the department dysfunction. He didn't want to go up for tenure in this environment."

Why do you have trouble getting along with Simon? "After I refused to back him on a hiring decision he started sending me emails, asking questions about some mistake I'd made, and then copying the whole department and the dean. He would send the same question over and over again to reinforce my perceived weakness."

Why did you get so emotional when you found Simon in Rachel's office? In timed-out mode, she might tell a story. "It reminded me of the time someone uprooted all the plants in my office. I can't prove it, but I know it was him."

Why don't you take action against Simon? "It's not like I haven't tried! I reported him once before, but no one took me seriously. So he's doing it again. But I've got my own research to do, and anyway, I don't get compensated for being chair. I just keep quiet because my time will soon be up. Let the next chair deal with it."

Rachel Nichols
Assistant Professor

Character Biography
Education: Ph.D. in Comparative Literature, U.C. Berkeley; MA in American Literature, Columbia University.

Teaches the following courses and seminars:
- 19th Century American Literature – Women Authors
- Introduction to American Studies
- Modern and Traditional Jewish-American Literature and Culture
- Louisa May Alcott: Radical Reformer and Children's Author
- Uncle Tom's Cabin Revisited

Publications include:
- "Louisa May Alcott: Radical Reformer and Children's Author," *American Quarterly*, June 2012.
- "The Scarlet Letter: The Puritan Mind in American Literature," *Journal of American Studies,* Sept 2013.
- "Lizzie Borden: Can this Legend be Axed?" *American Studies Journal*, May 2014.

Rachel came into academia later in life. She studied literature and American history in college and loved it, but married young and began raising a family right away, so didn't have much time to pursue higher education until her children were grown. She earned her master's degree while her children were in middle and high school. It was a huge struggle, and it made her very anxious and feeling like she had abandoned her home life for her own selfish needs. Her anxiety was compounded when her husband asked for a divorce.

With the kids finally out of the nest, she returned to school to earn her Ph.D. A favorite professor and mentor convinced her she'd make a great instructor, so she set aside her initial thoughts of publishing in order to pursue that career. Now she's finding that the politics of academia are sapping all the joy of teaching from her.

When she first began teaching, Simon was a huge help in getting her acclimated. He encouraged her to continue to write even while managing a large course load. His support and praise fed her depleted ego. They had coffee together frequently and enjoyed each other's company. She asked him to give her a lift to work one day when her car had a flat tire.

Simon took this as a sign that Rachel had deeper feelings for him. He began flirting with her at work and calling her at home at night just to talk. Uncomfortable with the attention, Rachel rebuffed him. Things have become very cool and uncomfortable and gradually more hostile over the past few months. Because she felt responsible for the change in their relationship, Rachel hasn't felt as though she could ask for help until the situation escalated to the point where the play begins.

Her primary source of support is her younger sister. Between the two of them, they share the burden of assisting their aging parents with financial and physical needs. Her phone calls are usually to her sister for advice or to talk about the parents. Occasionally her children call, but not often.

Talking Points
- She is afraid of Simon. "Everybody tells me I need to stand up to him. Maybe my vulnerability is why he's targeting me. He looks at me like he wants to kill me. It's like a horror movie where you meet the bully in the vegetable aisle at the supermarket. You look up from your shopping cart and there he is, staring at you."
- The tension is ruining her life. "I have nightmares. I've sought therapy. This is taking a huge toll on my personal and professional life."
- As a non-tenured professor, she doesn't want to raise a ruckus. "If you go up for tenure and have been less than compliant with the old guard, you're gone. It may not always happen that way, but the threat is there."
- To some degree she accepts the cultural perception that if you can't solve a problem on your own there must be something wrong with you. "What did I do to bring this on? Why am I the target?"
- But she is also angry about the cultural tendency to blame the victim. "It's like sitting in a room with a guy who sexually assaulted you. I know other people don't believe that. They tend to blame the victim—me. That's like blaming a woman who got raped."

Sample Talk-back Q and A's
What did Simon say in his emails? Derided her work as "American Studies Lite," trivia masquerading as scholarship, a thesis of no consequence, busywork masquerading as revisionism. "Everything that needs to be said about the Alcotts has already been said… better."

Why didn't you confront him about it? "I am definitely not the confrontational type. My family just didn't argue. I am conflict avoidant. Conflict makes my blood pressure rise."

How do you deal with the pressure? "I hide behind my office door. I come in early and leave late, trying to avoid running into him."

Why are you taking pills? In timed-in mode, the answer is "blood pressure." In timed-out mode, it's "panic attacks."

Why are you always texting or phoning someone? In timed-in mode, she would say it's something she has to check up on: a problem with a parent or other family member. In timed-out mode she might admit that it's actually a stress response to conflict, a way of being engaged elsewhere so she can avoid dealing with what's going on around her. She's probably calling someone in her support network: her mother or sister or best friend.

Dean Stone
Dean of the College of Liberal Arts and Interdisciplinary Studies

Backstory Notes
It is hinted in her CV that Dean Stone has a split in her life, having chosen academics over competitive sports. The athletic side of her enjoys competition, doesn't give in easily to men, and expects other women to be as powerful as she is. The academic side takes few chances and prefers sticking to a plan. In her personal life, she is single and still enjoys playing the field, although not within her department. Her daughter is in college and would like to play for the WNBA.

She has been dean for three years, during which time she has had to deal with the previous dean's abrupt departure, the sudden death of an elderly faculty member, and the pressure for layoffs in the college. Several male faculty members, including Simon, have courted her as a friend. She watches and plays sports that men play: golf, racquetball, and handball. She shoots and excels in archery. Her interest in "masculine" sports has been a useful social tool, but although she advocates for female equality in academia she has struggled to make women friends in the college. She wants to settle down and make friends, perhaps have a romance, but she has not developed these skills. She has been too busy pursuing other things.

She finds Dr. Albertson attractive and admires Carol for being gutsy and not letting people push her around. She judges Rachel harshly for getting such a late start on her career and wishes she would get a little backbone in the present situation. She remembers interviewing Emily but was not impressed with her style and now can't remember her name. She also disapproves of the way Emily is trying to rescue Rachel.

Talking Points
- The university has no policies on bullying, so there's no official guidance. The dean is on her own to deal with it as she sees fit, however imperfectly that may be.
- Chairs and deans receive no training on how to deal with reports of bullying, and this dean doesn't believe it would do any good anyway. "I would set up a training session, but faculty are very reluctant to participate in anything with the word 'training' in it. They think it's beneath them. If I made it a requirement, I'd be the bully."

Sample Talk-back Q and A's

Why don't you do something about Rachel's complaint? "No one around here seems to have the skills to have a meaningful conversation about resolving their own issues. They write mean emails and copy everyone up to the president. I don't want to get into these details. They want to call us and have us run their departments for them."

What do you suggest Rachel do? "People need to solve their own problems. Rachel should be more assertive. She should talk to the person she's having problems with, not complain to others. I have a lot more serious problems to deal with than these little department spats. I'm not going to take on her emotional stress or her crisis. I've got my own work to do."

Why do you take this so lightly instead of pushing it up through the system? In timed-in mode, she might say she wants to empower the women to take care of their own problems and issues. She doesn't like entitlement; she earned what she got and they can too. In timed-out mode, she might reveal that it's just too much trouble. Why should she care about these petty squabbles? She has important work of her own, better ways to spend her time.

4

Faculty Reflections

Faculty Reflections

Every discussion of academic bullying will be unique because of the range of experience, perspective, and personality that each participant brings to the table. We invited three UAA faculty members from three different disciplines to contribute reflections to this book, and as expected we got three very different responses.

E.J.R. David, Associate Professor of Psychology, discusses the way academic power structures mirror inequalities in the culture at large and how these cultures can normalize and nurture bullying behavior.

Osama Abaza, Professor of Civil Engineering, reflects on specific behaviors he has observed over a thirty-year career, and calls for universities to recognize the importance of collegiality and to actively and systematically promote it throughout their organizations.

Shawnalee Whitney, Associate Professor of Journalism and Communication, focuses on the personal and institutional costs of bullying and issues a call to action that includes structured approaches for targets, bystanders, departments, administrators, and institutions.

What Allows Bullying to Thrive in Academia?

Three Similarities Between Societal Oppression and Academic Bullying

By E. J. R. David

T he amount of bullying that goes on among both children and adults is troubling. According to research, more than 45% of the general population has experienced some form of it, and 35% have experienced it in the workplace (Hollis, 2012). Other research links bullying to a wide array of negative consequences in realms ranging from the social and occupational (e.g., isolation, poor job performance, burnout) to the psychological and physical (e.g., anxiety, depression, headaches, hypertension). For a review, see Cassell, 2011 or Keashly & Neuman, 2010. As bullying has become a national concern, the body of research has grown, guiding our approaches to bullying everywhere from our playgrounds and classrooms all the way to our workplaces and boardrooms.

Dr. E. J. R. David is Associate Professor of Psychology and Director of the Alaska Native Community Advancement in Psychology program at the University of Alaska Anchorage. He has published theoretical and empirical works on various forms of oppression, including two books: *Brown Skin, White Minds: Filipino -/ American Postcolonial Psychology* (2013) and *Internalized Oppression: The Psychology of Marginalized Groups* (2014). He has received Early Career Awards from the APA Minority Fellowship Program (2012) and the Asian American Psychological Association (2013) and a Cultural Humanitarian Award from the Alaska Psychological Association (2014). He was inducted as an AAPA Alaska Psychological Association Fellow in 2015 for his "unusual and outstanding contributions to Asian American Psychology."

Ironically, research shows bullying to be disturbingly rampant in the academic world as well—among academics and researchers themselves—where it sometimes goes by the name of academic incivility. One study reports that approximately 62% of people who work in higher education have experienced bullying at least once (Hollis, 2012). In another, 32% of university employees and 49% of faculty members reported bullying that lasted longer than three years (Keashly & Neuman, 2008). When half of all faculty members are experiencing long-term bullying in their workplaces, you know you have a serious problem.

Surprisingly, the greatest number of reports do not involve bullying between faculty and students but rather bullying within the faculty ranks: between faculty and their colleagues (especially senior colleagues) and administrators (many of whom also hold faculty rank). Indeed, Keashly & Neuman report that around 63% of the bullying that faculty members experienced originated with fellow faculty members.

Is there something about academia that makes it a particularly vulnerable setting for peer-to-peer bullying? If so, what characteristics of the academic world create the context in which bullying between faculty and administrators can thrive?

As I grappled with these questions, I began thinking about my own work on oppression, the various presentations of which (e.g., racial, cultural, gender, etc.) have been the central topic of my writings and teachings over the past sixteen years. I was reminded of the ways in which our society and its institutions tend to tolerate a wide range of oppression. In fact, our whole society seems to be a context in which oppression is not only allowed to survive, but also to adapt, evolve, and even increase.

There are three major factors that help to perpetuate society-level oppression. First, there are power differentials or inequalities between oppressor and oppressed. Second, oppression evolves over time to become more subtle and insidious, replacing overt institutional violence with a myriad of micro-aggressions. And finally, oppression survives and thrives in atmospheres of institutional or cultural "support" or "protection."

These three factors may be in play—to some extent and in some form—in the context of academic bullying as well. This essay will explore three characteristics of academia that may—however inadvertently—maintain, harbor, and reinforce bullying behavior between faculty members and between faculty and administrators.

Traditional Academic Power Structures Mirror Power Inequalities in the Larger Society

Oppression occurs when one group has more power, privilege, voice, representation, and access to resources than another group (or groups), and when such inequalities are used to maintain the status quo (i.e., domination of one group over another) (David & Derthick, 2014). Oppression is both a state and a process, with the state being the inequalities between groups and the process being how such inequalities are maintained by individual-level (e.g., prejudices) and institutional-level (e.g., policies) factors (Prilleltensky & Laurier, 1996). Just as people can be grouped in many different ways (e.g., by race, sex, sexual orientation, abilities, etc.), oppression based on group membership also comes in many different forms (e.g., racism, sexism, heterosexism, ableism, nativism or xenophobia, and others). Regardless of how people are grouped, the type of society that oppression both creates and maintains is characterized by a hierarchical, unequal power structure between the groups.

Academia has an undeniable hierarchical structure, with presidents, chancellors, vice chancellors, and provosts at the top; deans, directors, department chairs, and tenured professors somewhere in the middle; and untenured professors and staff near the bottom, directly above part-time instructors and adjuncts. Hierarchy comes with inherent power inequalities at all these levels. If bullying is the abuse of real or perceived power in order to force, threaten, coerce, intimidate, or dominate another person in a weaker or more vulnerable position, then it is easy to see how the conventional power structure can be fertile ground for bullying to occur. Indeed, because power difference is a key and defining feature of bullying, it is not surprising that research has found higher-level administrators (most of whom hold some form of faculty rank) and senior tenured professors to be most often identified as bullies (Keashly & Neuman, 2008).

In addition to the power structures themselves, we also need to look at who holds the highest-level positions in academia. More often than not, the higher education hierarchy closely resembles and reflects the unequal power structures that exist between different social groups in the larger society. In other words, people who are White, male, American, Christian, and heterosexual tend to dominate the higher-level positions and hold (or control) most of the power (Azziz, 2014). It is not too farfetched to expect the power differentials and perceived "weaknesses" of some groups (e.g., stereotypes) that are propagated in the larger society to creep into the world of academia and influence bullying behavior among faculty and higher administrators.

Indeed, research shows that those who are perceived to be weaker or more vulnerable tend to be the most common victims or targets of bullying in academia. Specifically, faculty who identify as immigrants, non-native English speakers, women, people of color, or lesbian, gay, bisexual, or transgender experience proportionally higher levels of bullying (Hollis, 2012). So here we see how oppression in the larger society—in the form of racism, sexism, heterosexism, along with the prejudices and stereotypes that drive them—can also come into play with bullying in academia.

Sophisticated Adults Tend to Create Sophisticated Bullying

Most people think of oppression in terms of overt, obvious, and clear examples that are primarily focused on racism (e.g., slavery, the Jim Crow era). In the contemporary United States, however, racism and other forms of social group oppression have evolved into more subtle, covert, or hidden forms (Sue, 2010). The prejudices and stereotypes that drive these oppressive practices may even be unknown, unconscious, or beyond intention and control (Banaji & Greenwald, 2013).

Many of today's oppressive attitudes, thoughts, feelings, and behaviors manifest as micro-aggressions. Micro-aggressions are brief and commonplace verbal, behavioral, and environmental indignities—whether intentional or unintentional—that communicate hostile, derogatory, or negative slights and insults to the target person or group (Sue, 2010). These seemingly harmless, "throwaway" remarks may insult, discount, or disparage a person on the basis of his or her
- ethnicity ('You're so articulate, you don't talk like a Black person at all.');
- gender ('You're too pretty to be a scientist.');
- sexual orientation ('That's so gay!');
- religion ('Merry Christmas!'); or
- national origin ('Immigrants are taking all the jobs!').

Just as societal-level oppression has grown less overt, so too has bullying. Classic bullying is typically characterized as violent, physically assaultive, and overtly intimidating; much modern-day bullying has evolved to become more subtle and covert (Rivera, 2011). In the academic workplace, subtle bullying may come in the form of interrupting the target during meetings, eye rolling when the target is speaking, undermining the target's credibility, and excluding the target from social conversations or other (informal or formal) gatherings. This is a more sophisticated form of bullying, common among adults, and perhaps most common among intelligent, highly-educated adults, the kind who make their careers in academia.

Contemporary bullies may not look like the classic stereotype of a bully either. The classic bully is typically characterized as a loner, a loser, someone with poor social skills who is also physically intimidating, mean, and/or angry. The sophisticated bully, on the other hand, can be likeable, humorous, attractive, popular, and high achieving: a success in the academic world and beyond. Charismatic bullies do not rely on physical force to intimidate or overpower their targets, but instead use subtle, smooth, undetected manipulation to exert their power (real or perceived) over others (Rivera, 2011). We can easily see this type of bully among adults, especially highly intelligent adults. Charismatic bullies are likely to be leaders whose charm and popularity make it difficult for others to see them as bullies (Rivera, 2011).

The micro-aggressive behaviors and sophisticated forms of bullying that are practiced by charismatic bullies help to maintain the imbalanced power structure that exists in academia, which can then breed even more bullying behaviors. Over the years, academic bullying has evolved into something smooth and subtle and acceptable, allowing it to survive almost undetected, except by its victims.

Academic Culture Can Minimize, Normalize, and Inadvertently Reinforce Bullying

According to the growing body of literature on workplace bullying, an organization's culture and climate strongly influence the extent to which hostile behaviors are allowed to occur or thrive. Organizational culture and climate influence how members define and perceive the nature of interpersonal interaction as well as how they respond and manage such interactions (Lester, 2009). Unfortunately, the culture in higher education seems to be highly amenable to normalization, tolerance, acceptance, and minimization of micro-aggressions or sophisticated forms of bullying.

Research shows that organizational cultures and climates where bullying flourishes tend to be competitive, adversarial, and politicized, characteristics that most academics will recognize from their own workplaces. It is common for professors—especially non-tenured ones—to be socialized with the idea that "You're supposed to be stressed out; that's the job!" (Anonymous Academics, 2014). The culture tolerates such a variety of undermining, micro-aggressive, and passive-aggressive behaviors (e.g., indirectly threatening a colleague's professional status, subtly ignoring a peer's contributions, gossiping about a colleague, using humor to belittle a fellow faculty member, and many others) that some writers have even described the academic workplace as operating under a "culture of cruelty" (Farley & Sprigg, 2014).

Other research suggests that when targets of workplace bullying choose to do something about it, only about 7% of the cases result into some form of a negative sanction against the bully (e.g., censure, transfer, or termination). In other cases, the perpetrator's supervisors directly helped the bully or punished the target (42%), the bully's supervisor did nothing to intervene (40%), the organization's human resources office supported the bully or did nothing (32%), or the target's colleagues sided with the bully (11%) (Danie, 2008).

Many institutions try to cope with bullies by waiting them out or ignoring the problem (Hollis, 2012). Consistent with—and perhaps because of—this, research suggests that faculty who were targets of bullying were more likely to talk to the union (31%) or a lawyer (15%), rather than to seek help from university-based avenues such as higher administrators or human resources officers (28%) (McKay et al., 2008). The reasons for the low rate of "help-seeking" from the university is likely due to fear or mistrust of the university itself. Indeed, when asked if they had reported the bullying to university officials, 49% of faculty respondents said, "No, I do not think it would make a difference," and 29% said, "No, I think it would negatively impact my job" (McKay et al., 2008).

These data suggest that a culture that normalizes bullying may also be a culture of mistrust. When ineffective and unsupportive university actions (or inactions) are combined with low expectations and mistrust, the message is that bullying has no consequences. Is it any wonder that bullying might thrive in a work environment like this?

The Similarities Don't End Here

Sadly, the similarities between larger societal oppression and academic bullying do not end here. Oppression in all its many forms (racism, sexism, heterosexism, etc.) produces a myriad of well-documented negative effects on marginalized peoples' economic, social, psychological, and physical well-being. Similarly, the emerging literature on bullying in higher education suggests that it frequently leads to anxiety, sleep disturbances, burnout, paranoia, headaches, alcohol use, increased heart rate, hypertension, anger, and depression. Struggling with these issues may adversely affect the personal and occupational functioning of a large number of our fellow faculty members (e.g., Cassell, 2011; Keashly & Neuman, 2010).

Clearly, we need to address larger societal oppression in a complex manner, with at least one eye toward how existing systems and institutions may be harboring oppression and another eye toward how modern-day oppression has evolved to become more subtle. Similarly, we also need a much more nuanced and realistic understanding of academic bullying behaviors, how they have evolved toward subtlety over time, and how our traditional academic institutions and cultures may reinforce, protect, and even facilitate these behaviors.

Awareness is a necessary step in addressing any kind of oppression. First, we need to recognize that a problem exists, know what it looks like, and understand its source. Then we need to become motivated and to develop the political and moral will to effect real change. There are many steps to this process and plenty of directions to take, from individual acts of micro-resistance to policy changes at the administrative level. The parallels between larger societal oppression and bullying in academia provide us with a clearer lens with which to see the problem of faculty bullying. With this lens, perhaps our solutions will be more clear and effective.

References

Anonymous Academics. "Bullying in academia: 'Professors are supposed to be stressed! That's the job.'" *The Guardian*, Higher Education Network, October 24, 2014.

Azziz, Ricardo. "Back to the Future: Why Is the Diversity of University Leadership Stuck in the '80s?" *Huffington Post* website, June 24, 2014.

Banaji, Mahzarin R. and Anthony G. Greenwald. *Blind Spot: Hidden Biases of Good People.* New York: Delacorte Press, 2013.

Cassell, Macgorine. A. "Bullying in Academe: Prevalent, Significant, and Incessant." *Contemporary Issues in Education Research,* 4(5), 2011.

David, E. J. R., & Annie O. Derthick. "What is internalized oppression, and so what?" *Internalized Oppression: The Psychology of Marginalized Groups.* E.J.R. David, Editor. New York: Springer Publishing, 2014.

Farley, Sam and Christine Sprigg. "Culture of cruelty: why bullying thrives in higher education." *The Guardian,* Higher Education Network. November 3, 2014.

Hollis, Leah. P. *Bully in the Ivory Tower: How Aggression and Incivility Erode American Higher Education.* Wilmington, Delaware: Patricia Berkly LLC, 2012.

Keashly, Loraleigh and Joel H. Neuman. "Faculty Experiences with Bullying in Higher Education: Causes, Consequences, and Management." *Administrative Theory & Praxis,* 32(1), March 2010.

---. "Final Report: Workplace Behavior (Bullying) Project Survey." Minnesota State University-Mankato, 2008.

Lester, Jaime. "Not Your Child's Playground: Workplace Bullying Among Community College Faculty." *Community College Journal of Research and Practice,* 33(5), 2009.

McKay, Ruth, Diane H. Arnold, Jae Fratzl, and Roland Thomas. "Workplace Bullying in Academia: A Canadian Study." *Employee Responsibilities and Rights Journal,* 20(2), 2008.

Namie, Gary. "U.S. Hostile Workplace Survey 2000." *Workplace Bullying Institute,* 2008.

Prilleltensky, Isaac and Lev Gonick. "Polities Change, Oppression Remains: On the Psychology and Politics of Oppression." *International Society of Political Psychology,* 17. March 1996.

Rivera, David. "Bullying and Microaggressions. Bullying: More than physical violence." *Psychology Today*, January 23, 2011.

Sue, Derald Wing, Editor. *Microaggressions and Marginality: Manifestations, Dynamics, and Impact.* Hoboken, New Jersey: John Wiley and Sons, 2010.

Collegiality and Toxic Behavior
Reflections from a Senior Faculty Member and Administrator

By Osama A. Abaza

Collegiality is an essential component of an academic institution that hopes to provide a high quality education. Collegiality creates an environment of mutual support and respect that is important in our interactions with each other and in the models we provide for our students. A professional collaborative environment allows individuals to excel in their fields and to find both personal and professional fulfillment. Academic development and personal growth for educators translates into a better quality of education for students. Simply put, universities perform better when members of staff and faculty work together as a coherent team.

Dr. Osama A. Abaza is Professor of Civil Engineering at the University of Alaska Anchorage (UAA). He has over thirty years of experience in the field of civil/transportation engineering and has produced more than sixty-three peer-reviewed publications. In addition to his faculty position, he has served as Department Chair, Dean of the College of Engineering, and Vice President for Administrative Affairs. Honors include the UAA Chancellor's Award for Excellence in Service to the Community (2013) and the Institute of Transportation Engineers' (ITE) Engineer of the Year award (2012).

A collegial atmosphere is one in which faculty and staff display respect and courtesy to their colleagues, from simple gestures that signify regard to assistance with research and other professional projects. The practice of accepting and sharing responsibility for creating a productive workplace derives from how well each member of the community carries his or her own fair share of the common workload (Cipriano, 2011). These elements lie at the heart of successful interactions in academic life.

Collegiality can be damaged or destroyed in environments that are marked by negativity and tension, where personal battles take a toll on productivity. Environments toxic to collegiality exist wherever individuals are allowed to use unethical, unprofessional, and even illegal means to manipulate and inconvenience those around them. Workplace bullies are generally very skilled at these behaviors. They are often motivated by personal gain, and they seek to maintain or increase their power, money, and influence. They intentionally divert attention from their performance shortfalls and failures. They do not recognize their obligations to the organization in which they work, nor do they display ethical and professional conduct to their colleagues. They define relationships with co-workers not by organizational structure, but by those they favor and those they don't

(Benoit 2011). They may also harbor resentments based on gender, race, educational level, background, and many other factors.

Toxic behaviors are often associated with the inability to accept responsibility for actions, feelings, needs, and problems that stem from deep wounding within an individual (Chernoff et al., 2015). I've seen this dynamic play out time and again in my own personal experience. Workplace bullies take no responsibility for their attitudes and behaviors and often exhibit almost a complete lack of self-control. Unaddressed emotional pain causes them to spread their pain to others around them; their unhealthy coping strategies create new problems for those who must try to work with them.

Most academic institutions struggle at least occasionally with some version of diminishing resources, budget cutting, and even program cutting. These conditions place a tremendous strain on relationships amongst faculty and administrators. When the actions of individual faculty members are divisive, uncompromising, and inflexible, the strain is further increased. The morale of a whole department can be eroded when one or more members accept a significantly lower degree of responsibility than their peers for achieving a shared purpose.

Having served as a department chair, dean, and vice president at multiple institutions over the past three decades, I have had opportunities to observe a wide range of toxic behaviors in the halls of higher education. Here are four that I have found to be especially common, all of which I believe are rooted in personal distress that has not been appropriately addressed.

Deception and hearsay. A person whose past is full of unaddressed emotional distress may have a certain eagerness to share that anguish with others. On the other hand, mature adults who are focused on bettering themselves do not need to act maliciously toward their peers. Circulating hearsay and deception which result in confusion and distress for others can help the malefactors feel like they're not the only ones in pain.

Envy. Workplace bullies can be acutely sensitive to the achievements of others and may resent the successes of their colleagues. They do not celebrate their colleagues' accomplishments, nor do they applaud emotional stability; instead, they are envious of it. Their own failure to respond to setbacks with resilience may cause them to resent others who have mastered that seemingly impossible task. I have seen cases in which a single researcher claimed credit for breakthroughs achieved by an entire team and others in which a faculty member used personal connections to bypass departmental policies in pursuit of an individual agenda. Others might steal intellectual property or negate a colleague's contribution in order to get ahead of someone they envy.

Denial or transference of responsibility. Workplace bullies may have trouble dealing with a wide array of negative emotions. Their inability to deal with failure and feelings of humiliation may come into play when they make mistakes as, sooner or later, everyone does. They may or may not realize that they made the mistake, but in either case, when it is brought to their attention they refuse to admit to it. The situation becomes more toxic with increased confrontation. When others try to provide constructive criticism, they respond with dissension, deflection, and denial. In addition, because of their need to be at the center of attention, workplace bullies have a way of shifting the focus of any conversation onto themselves. Even if they thereby victimize themselves, they win by at least earning the attention of others (Chernoff et al., 2015).

Manipulation. People who haven't effectively dealt with their own weaknesses often feel a shaky sense of control over themselves and their emotions. They may compensate by seeking greater control over other aspects of their lives and especially over the behavior of those around them. By manipulating others, they feel a greater sense of control over those people. This seems to give them a sense of satisfaction and fills an emotional void in their lives. I've seen individuals in hiring positions take advantage of their positions of power, expecting or demanding certain favors and special treatment from those who "owe" them for securing their jobs. When department chairs rotate frequently (as they do at my current institution), it can be very difficult to resist attempted manipulations from colleagues who may soon be in a position to retaliate. I have been in this situation myself: been that new hire, resisted that attempted manipulation, and experienced retaliation in the form of toxic behaviors directed at me in public. None of this had anything to do with the job I was hired to perform, but all of it interfered with my ability to do that job and to devote my full attention to doing it well.

Toward a More Collegial Institution

Two years ago, I approached our teaching and learning center, the Center for Advancing Faculty Excellence (CAFE), to help us tackle these issues university-wide. The Center sponsored a faculty learning community, which met over a semester to discuss a book (*Facilitating a Collegial Department in Higher Education*) and to generate ideas for promoting a collegial working environment on our campus. I led this discussion group. Our recommendations appear in Resources, page 120.

Several of us were especially interested in the role that faculty leaders can and should play in promoting collegiality. One of the *Toxic Friday* performances was held specifically for department chairs, deans, and directors with faculty supervisory responsibilities. Resources of particular interest to faculty leaders include "20 Steps Chairs Can Take" (Cipriano, pp. 56-60) and "Concrete Steps for Chairs" (Chu, pp. 77-79). Well-chosen team-building exercises can also contribute to a greater sense of departmental collaboration and collegiality.

Through these and other workshops and activities, my colleagues and I took that critical first step of acknowledgement. We began on a small scale what the institution must continue on a larger one: to recognize and define the extent of the problem and then to develop a system-wide strategy for addressing it. That strategy should include, among other things,

- an awareness campaign;
- systems of policy-making and target- and goal-setting; and
- working plans to deal with toxic behavior at all levels of the institution.

Higher education is not immune to workplace bullying; we have a substantial number of toxic behavior cases right here on our campuses. Collegiality is too important to be taken for granted. We must be proactive in reducing toxic behavior in our academic departments and on our campuses. The worst thing we can do is wait until a major incident forces us to respond.

References

Benoit, Suzanne. "Surviving a Toxic Workplace Without Losing Your Mind." Benoit Consulting, November 7, 2011.

Chernoff, Marc, Angel Chernoff and Kathy Caprino. "12 Toxic Behaviors That Push People Away From You." *The Open Mind* website, March 17, 2015.

Chu, Don. *The Department Chair Primer: What Chairs Need to Know and Do to Make a Difference.* Jossey Bass, 2012.

Cipriano, Robert and Jeffrey Buller. *Facilitating a Collegial Department in Higher Education: Strategies for Success.* Jossey-Bass, 2011.

Don't Just Stand There. Do Something!
Responding to Faculty Bullying in Higher Education

By Shawnalee A. Whitney

T he focus of this piece, as the title implies, is to get people to do something about workplace bullying in higher education. By 'people' I don't mean the targets, those who are suffering abuse at the hands of their colleagues. Let me be clear: the targets do not bear the responsibility for solving this problem. Many, and perhaps most, of them are in positions of vulnerability; they may be the

Shawnalee Whitney is Associate Professor of Journalism and Communication and Interim Director of the Center for Advancing Faculty Excellence at the University of Alaska Anchorage. She started teaching at the college level in 1986 and has been affiliated with six different institutions over a thirty-year career.

ones least able to respond. But there are many others—senior faculty members, chairs, deans, human resources leaders, and others up the academic chain of command—who are positioned to respond both formally and informally to situations involving abuse by and of faculty members.

Even in the best circumstances, it is a challenge to genuinely understand and empathize with another person's experience. It is even more difficult when that experience is emotionally uncomfortable, politically charged, or otherwise outside our comfort zone. The complex and challenging situations involved in workplace bullying can leave reasonable, intelligent, and even highly decisive and articulate people seemingly frozen, unsure of what to say, unable to process, and all but unable to respond effectively. Being stuck in this way—unable or unwilling to respond—has consequences. Workplace bullying that goes unchecked simply continues, sometimes for years, and at substantial cost to individuals, departments, and institutions.

This essay provides a glimpse into the experience of the faculty member as a target, discusses the role of bystander or observer, and includes recommendations for various personal and institutional responses. It is informed by my own experiences as well as literature reviews and explorations of this subject. I hope my perspective and ideas may help you and your institution become better equipped to deal with this expensive and damaging problem.

Background

I used to believe that workplace bullying was an aberration, an occasional or unusual disruption in the normal state of collegial relationships that adults could expect in their professional lives. I expected the academic world to be a particularly safe place in this regard, filled as it is with smart people dedicated to searching for better ways to do things.

Today, however, I am less naïve about the nature of the professional contexts in which I have spent my adult life. My perspective has changed after working through the literature and sitting in the front row for more than one instance of bullying. I now understand that workplace bullying is more widespread and causes more damage than many of us would like to think. While I still believe that collegial professional environments are possible, I now know that there are specific steps we can and must take if we are to achieve them.

It is the cumulative weight, the daily grind, the overall wear and tear of email after email, comment after comment, interaction after interaction, that takes its toll on targets.

These are not just my particular experiences and opinions; a substantial body of evidence supports them. Researchers Namie and Namie established the Workplace Bullying Institute (WBI) in 1997 and have developed a growing body of evidence that demonstrates the seriousness of this problem nationwide. Other researchers have focused specifically on the higher education environment (see especially Keashly & Newman, 2010). According to Hollis (2012), the incidence of workplace bullying in higher education is a surprising 58% higher than it is for other workplace settings.

Significantly, the first word in the WBI's definition of bullying is 'repeated.' Over time, a series of even low-level annoyances can have a cumulative adverse effect that is significantly more damaging than any single instance of the behavior. Edwards and Greenberg (2010) call this *insidious workplace behavior*: "a form of intentionally harmful workplace behavior that is legal, subtle, and low-level (rather than severe), repeated over time, and directed at individuals and organizations…subtle and stealthy behavior that cumulatively chips away at a worker's dignity."

Sometimes the difficulty is not in getting through a particular, extreme moment of abuse, but in the cumulative power of the behavior over time. An administrator might not see the problem based on the wording of just one email. But it is not just one. It is the cumulative weight, the daily grind, the overall wear and tear of email after email, comment after comment, interaction after interaction, that takes its toll on targets.

Costs

Substantial numbers of higher education faculty members report being bullied, and many of them (63.4%) say that their colleagues are the perpetrators. Student-perpetrated acts of violence may get the most public attention, but ironically they are not the professoriate's greatest area of concern. Faculty members express greater levels of concern about workplace harassment coming from colleagues—particularly senior colleagues—and superiors (Keashly & Newman, 2008).[1]

There's no question that the experience of workplace bullying leads to reduced job satisfaction and organizational commitment on the part of the target. Faculty members who are targets quickly lose any satisfaction or joy that might come from being a part of a vibrant campus community. In time, targeted professors may even begin to dread being on campus. And can you blame them? Would you want to come to campus knowing you'll almost certainly be on the receiving end of barbed comments, hurtful emails, and more?

If the situation is ongoing, targeted faculty members might adapt their own behaviors to reduce the impact on the health and safety of the workplace. In one instance I know of, when it became clear that those in authority were not going to offer meaningful assistance, several faculty members restructured their schedules, coming in for office hours or course preparation at times when the bully was known to be in class or away from campus. Others began keeping office doors partially or completely closed. These strategies might have afforded a modicum of protection from the bully, but they also reduced availability to students and made the department look uninviting and inaccessible.

Other adaptive behaviors can harm the target's professional reputation, erode his or her confidence and dignity, and reduce interactions with other more positive colleagues. Yes, the target can adapt and pull back, but doing so merely sets the target up for pain of a different sort. It's a Catch 22.

For example, for junior faculty members, withdrawal and avoidance strategies will almost certainly work against their pursuit of tenure. In the *Toxic Friday* video, the more senior members of the department clearly have a sense of what's going on—two of them have been targeted by Simon in the past—but they seem to be overlooking or denying what Simon's bullying behavior is costing them as a department. In fact, not one but two junior faculty members look like they might consider leaving. Statistically, that's not at all unlikely.

Many of those who face workplace bullying do leave, even if it's difficult to do so and even if it means doing damage to their own professional standing. In most cases—61%—it is the target and not the perpetrator/bully that ends up quitting (29%), being forced out (19%), or being fired (13%). According to the WBI, the perpetrator is adversely influenced only 25% of the time (2014).

---

[1] "Workplace Bullying: An Integrative Literature Review" offers a strong broad-based exploration of bullying types and their personal and organizational impacts (Bartlett & Bartlett, 2011).

Hollis (2012) estimates that the cost of recruiting and replacing a faculty member is about 150 percent of his or her annual salary. Clearly, the focus should be on developing, retaining, and helping new faculty hires to become more fully grounded in the institution in order to advance the field of study and contribute to the success of students. It should not be on having to start the process anew due to bullying or mobbing by other faculty members.

There are long-term image costs associated with having faculty members leave your institution due to workplace bullying. Part of these individuals' stories will undoubtedly be how ineffective your institution's response was. Their stories can detract from your institution's academic reputation and make it that much more difficult to recruit and retain other faculty members in the future.

Targeted faculty members who, for personal or professional reasons, choose not to leave risk serious damage to their physical health and emotional well-being. Prolonged exposure to workplace bullying results in a range of stress-related diseases and health complications (WBI, 2015). Cardiovascular problems, adverse neurological changes, gastrointestinal problems, and immunological impairment represent the tip of the iceberg. This list mirrors the experiences I have had and situations other faculty members have shared with me. I know colleagues who have gained weight, lost weight, suffered stomach problems, suffered cardiac problems, had trouble with their skin, and much more. A faculty member's physical health is very much at risk when he or she becomes the target of a workplace bully.

The WBI (2015) reports that workplace bullying adversely influences psychological well-being as well, causing debilitating anxiety (experienced by 80% of targets), panic attacks (52%), clinical depression (49%), and post-traumatic stress disorder (30%), among other things. Targeted faculty members report feelings of anxiety and even panic at the sound of the bully's voice in the hallway or the thought of driving toward campus.

The cumulative weight of this trauma should not be underestimated: in one survey, 29% of targets said they had contemplated suicide and 16% said they had developed a plan to take their life (WBI, 2012). A longitudinal study by the Bergen Bullying Research Group concluded that the odds of suicidal ideation by those previously bullied was *twice* the likelihood of those who had not experienced bullying (Nielsen et al., 2015).[2]

Administrators with financial responsibilities to the institution should be advised: failure to put a stop to bullying will almost certainly result in higher costs for faculty health care and insurance.

---

2 The asphyxiation of United Kingdom academic Dr. Stefan Grimm is one recent example of a suicide widely attributed to workplace mistreatment (Frood, 2015). Sadly, his death is not an isolated incident. The website of the Workplace Bullying Institute cites other instances, including one case from a corporate setting where the target's loved ones ultimately earned a settlement of $10 million. In Australia, government officials decided to advance a nationwide anti-bullying initiative in 2012 in no small part due to the number of people lost to suicide. In 2012, Australia had 2,500 suicides, including 450 by children. Eighty percent of these cases included bullying as a factor.

Bystander Trauma

Targets aren't the only ones who get hurt. Colleagues who sit alongside them in meetings as bystanders and observers may suffer negative consequences, too. Bystander trauma is gaining attention in a range of fields, and some researchers argue that stresses or traumas associated with "being victimized by, engaging in, or witnessing unethical behavior" all have negative consequences (Giacalone & Promislo, 2010).

The *Toxic Friday* target spends a great deal of time in conversation with others, worrying about the bully and what he will do next. Her department colleagues seem supportive, and two of them have even had similar experiences at the hands of the very same perpetrator, but they are either unwilling to speak up (Charles) or ineffective when they do (Carol, the chair).

Failed attempts at intervention can have physical and emotional consequences for bystanders similar to those for targets. I entered one of these situations myself when I first noticed the tensions in a meeting and assumed they must be the result of a backstory that pre-dated my arrival. Over time, as the manifestations of bullying became more frequent and overt, I realized the situation was far more complex. It was a sick, helpless feeling to recognize that abuse was happening but not know how to respond to it.

The silent scene in the video—the one where the clock is ticking as conversations go on and on about the situation—dramatizes the loss of time and productivity that results from being caught up in a situation of this nature. Even if you think you are seeing or hearing a great deal of concern voiced about the alleged bully, it is likely that the target is sharing only a small portion of what he or she is managing internally. A conversation of just fifteen or twenty minutes with you might represent many sleepless nights and many waking hours the target has spent thinking and talking about it. In all likelihood, the pain has lasted much longer and the emotional suffering runs much deeper than you—and perhaps even the target—may realize.

What Doesn't Work and Why

Toxic Friday's bullying target Rachel is experiencing many of the negative outcomes detailed above. The quality of her work is being questioned; her confidence in it and in herself is suffering; her physical and emotional health seems to be compromised; and the time she spends with others in the workplace (the dean, the chair, other colleagues) often focuses on the distressing situation with Simon, the bully, rather than on her research or her professional efforts in teaching, learning, and promoting student success. Fear of retaliation, lack of administrative support, and an absence of clear policies on campus bullying keep many people like Rachel from seeking assistance (Clark et al., 2013).

It is not enough merely to determine who is being bullied and why, or to assume that these situations will work themselves out if only the targets will toughen up, as *Toxic Friday's* Charles suggests. Those treatments are deeply flawed because of the simple but uncomfortable fact that some faculty members are more likely to be targeted than others.

The book *Workplace Bullying* (particularly in Chapter 2) offers a strong exploration of groups that are most likely to be targeted (Rayner et al., 2001). A few pages ago, my colleague E. J. R. David discussed some ways academic bullying mirrors societal level oppression, particularly in the choice of targets (see page 91).

It is important to identify categories of those most likely to be bullied, but it does not solve the problem. Researchers Namie and Namie describe a common perception that "there must be something about the targeted person to warrant uninvited psychological assaults against them…[The victims] did something to provoke the bully's reaction, or their personality made them prone to targethood." The researchers conclude—and I concur—that this is nonsense. If one person is being abusive toward another, someone must move in. Failure to do so creates even greater injury.

You might be surprised by the kinds of ineffectual comments that are sometimes offered in place of action to those voicing concern about faculty mistreatment and bullying.

- "We've known about this problem for some time; wish we could do something about it."
- "If there was some official record of the problem, we could take action."
- "This sort of thing happens in departments across campus."
- "Who started this? What started this? What's REALLY going on there?"
- "There are two sides to every story. What did you do to bring this on yourself?"
- "Why don't you just tell X to f*#& off?"
- "We have a clear policy on bullying. We don't tolerate it."
- "There's got to be some reaction other than fear. You're not really 'afraid.'"

Responses like these do nothing to address the problem. In the words of Desmond Tutu, "If you are neutral in situations of injustice, you have chosen the side of the oppressor. If an elephant has its foot on the tail of a mouse…the mouse will not appreciate your neutrality."

Learning from Others

The situation is not hopeless. There are a variety of specific things we can and must do to address the problem of faculty-to-faculty bullying.

First, we need to learn from others who have tackled the problem. Think about the many anti-bullying campaigns that have been advanced in K-12 education. Most people would be outraged if a teacher or principal said something like, "We know that Child X is being bullied, but there's nothing we can do about it." Yet that is precisely the sort of position that is taken again and again on college campuses as professional environments.

Schools and communities understand the damage that bullying causes. They have identified behaviors that are hurtful, and developed strategies for calling bullies out when they cross the line. The responses, standards, policies, and methods are both normative and procedural. Normative approaches include classroom discussions of appropriate behavior that teach children how to respond on behalf of themselves or their peers.

Procedural approaches provide specific steps that must be taken or sanctions that must be imposed so that the response is immediate and institutionalized.

Both of these ideas could be used in higher education. Normatively, faculty members could meet at department- or college-level gatherings to discuss and identify basic expectations of collegial relationships and interactions. These *Toxic Friday* resources are designed to facilitate normative discussions. Procedurally, you could familiarize yourself with any relevant policies or procedures that may exist: in faculty contracts, human resources handbooks, even in state or local law (some departments of education have guidelines for ethical behavior, codes of conduct, and so on in their states). These documents can offer insights into what should happen procedurally if there is a problem. It's better to have a procedure and not need it than to need it and have a series of administrators tell you, "I'm not really sure what we're expected to do in a case like this."

Would faculty members on your campus know where to turn if they were feeling miserable at work or suffering physical and emotional damage as a result of their interactions with colleagues?

We can also look to fellow colleges and universities for models and procedures. Many campuses have pathways for expressing concern about inappropriate student behavior that could be adapted for expressing problems with colleagues as well. In the wake of the 2007 Virginia Tech shooting, many institutions created *care teams*, groups that communicate with one another if a student is exhibiting unexpected or inappropriate behavior outside of normal ranges. Care teams typically receive reports, check in on students in a variety of ways, and mobilize appropriate responses when there are points of deep concern.

Thankfully, with a couple of fairly high profile exceptions, there have been relatively few instances of faculty-on-faculty physical violence[3], so a large, multi-member care and response team may not be necessary. But there are still lessons to be learned from this model. Junior faculty members in particular may suffer in silence, with no one to contact if they're feeling embattled. Would faculty members on your campus know where to turn if they were feeling miserable at work or suffering physical and emotional damage as a result of their interactions with colleagues? The department chair may be the right starting point for some, but it will depend entirely on your structure for evaluation, retention, tenure, and so on. Faculty unions are another option, but as *Toxic Friday's* department chair Carol notes, they aren't always the best choice. Other options include charging an ombuds office with management of these kinds of issues. No matter where the resource is housed, faculty members should know that there is someone available to them and that their concerns will be respectfully heard.

---

[3] The most high profile instance of faculty-on-faculty violence is likely the case of Dr. Amy Bishop, an assistant professor at the University of Alabama Huntsville, who took the lives of three faculty members and wounded three others in a shooting that took place in a department meeting.

Taking Action: Structured Approaches

Appropriate responses are everyone's responsibility.

Targets

A target's number one responsibility is his or her own safety, health, and emotional well-being. If you ever find yourself in this situation, you may want to avoid isolated interactions with the bully, particularly if you are beginning to feel fearful around him or her. Watch for problematic behavior to surface in a group setting (such as in a department meeting), and respond to it there.

An approach known as *perception checking* can be very useful. It consists of three dimensions: 1) identification of the behavior you noticed; 2) coming up with at least two possible interpretations of the behavior; and 3) asking for clarification from the other person. If you practice this a few times in non-threatening situations with family and friends, then it will be easier to use quickly in more charged moments.

For instance, assume that you asked a question about a course scheduled for the next academic year and, in response, the bully sighed, looked at the clock, and rolled his eyes. Right in that moment, you might say, "Dr. Smith, I noticed you sighed and rolled your eyes. I'm wondering whether you think we've already addressed this question, or are you thinking that the meeting is running too long?" This may seem difficult and/or uncomfortable, but it identifies the behavior in a public way and puts Dr. Smith on notice.

Bystanders and observers

Bystanders, particularly those in senior and tenured positions, can play a pivotal role in bullying situations (Lutgen-Sandvik & Fletcher, 2013), and any of us may become a bystander at any time. Each of us must take our own measure of responsibility for creating and maintaining a healthy academic culture. We must set positive examples, model good behavior, and speak up more readily when we witness instances of abuse.

Practicing a few basic intervention strategies can help us develop the skills and confidence to step up in the moment. The perception checking process could come in handy here as well. A bystander might say, "I noticed you were sighing and rolling your eyes when Professor X was speaking. That's not the professional behavior we expect in our meetings. Do you have an issue with what she was saying, or were you just thinking the meeting was running too long?"

Occasionally, a bystander might need to invite a colleague into his or her office for a private chat. David Yamada of the New Workplace Institute recommends that such conversations involve the alleged bully and two others, but not the target. It is important to record the time, date, and nature of these conversations.

Departments

Talk about these issues before they become problems. Perhaps you've watched other departments on your campus implode, and you thought, "I hope that never happens to us." Maybe you even felt relieved that it was happening to them and not to you. But those departments may have been secure, functional workplaces at one point, too.

Simply put, hope is not a plan. Given the prevalence of workplace bullying, even departments that enjoy good working relationships and positive climates must pay attention if they wish to remain bully-free zones. If you believe there's a problem with bullying in your department, consider bringing in a neutral third party to help you establish a policy or set of procedures that could be used to shut it down, even in a situation where it is ongoing. You may also want to create a code of conduct for departmental interactions. Your student code of conduct or relevant disciplinary or professional codes might be good places to start.

Campuses that don't have clear and reliable policies, procedures, and identifiable resources are doing more than failing: they're actually contributing to a climate and pattern of hostility that is known to invoke harm.

Administrators

It is absolutely critical for department chairs, deans, human resources personnel, and others in positions of authority to respond in a timely and structured way. Campuses that don't have clear and reliable policies, procedures, and identifiable resources are doing more than failing: they're actually contributing to a climate and pattern of hostility that is known to invoke harm. When approached with a claim of bullying, administrators should not simply say the first thing that comes into their minds. It doesn't matter what they personally think, or how they themselves would respond, or if they're uncomfortable with the whole idea of bullying. They are being paid to manage difficult situations in an even-handed and professional manner, and they have a responsibility to do it well.[4]

A structured approach serves everyone well. Development of appropriate policies and a clear process for registering complaints should involve a range of parties: human resources personnel, compliance officers, legal counsel, administrators, and union officials (if they are part of the campus structure). Faculty should be involved, too, to ensure that the needs of targets are met. Anti-bullying policies and procedures must consider the

---

[4] Oddly, it is not uncommon for workplace bullies to report that they themselves are being bullied. Bullies will sometimes issue a preemptive strike by going to an authority figure to allege mistreatment by their targets. Yamada (2013) and DePietro & Buddie (2014) have both reported on this tendency, and there is no denying it is a complicating factor. Reports of this nature should not, however, be an excuse for administrators to throw up their hands and say, "We'll never sort this out." It's better to have a clear, even-handed, reliable process in place and use it, trusting that an appropriate investigation of claims will bring some degree of clarity. Targets may be quite distressed by having a bully level accusations at them, but their concerns may be allayed if systems seem clear and reliable and if the larger campus culture is one that does not support bullying.

unique features of faculty labor dynamics. Faculty in tenured or tenure-track positions may have complicated review and evaluation relationships. Departments may consist of tenured faculty co-existing in decades-long relationships, term faculty with uncertain employment situations, adjunct faculty who teach only term by term, and more.[5]

With a protocol in place, the dean (or other administrator) has a reliable place to start. Specific but neutral questions invite the faculty member to explain the nature and scope of the situation, including names, key behaviors and issues, how long it has been going on, and how much time they have spent thinking and worrying about it. Targeted faculty members may have tried to increase their sense of safety and security by taking self-defense classes, installing peepholes in their doors, or otherwise demonstrating significant levels of hyper-vigilance. You may be surprised to learn how much faculty energy and how many personal and institutional resources are being devoted to each toxic situation.

Sample Intake Questions

- What kinds of verbal behaviors have made you feel targeted?
- What kinds of nonverbal behaviors have made you feel targeted?
- What sorts of behaviors or actions are you using to manage the situation?
- Have you changed your behaviors to manage the way you interact with this colleague?
- Do you know if anyone else has taken similar action?
- Do you feel in danger physically, emotionally, professionally, or in any other way?
- If I were to approach your colleague what do you think he/she would tell me about this situation? What about other members of your department?
- What is the outcome you wish to achieve? How would this situation look if it was "solved?"
- Are you aware that _____ is available as a resource on our campus for those who believe they have been bullied? Have you been in touch with them?
- What questions do you have for me?

Institutions

Identify appropriate policies and procedures. If your institution doesn't yet have these, it's time to create them. Develop a clear, reliable intake process that standardizes the response and demonstrates to the complainant that his or her concern will be taken seriously and handled professionally. There are a variety of bullying-related intake forms online that could be altered to meet the needs of your particular campus or situation. Create care teams or some other clearly identifiable, reliable pathways for faculty members and employees to get help if they believe they are being harmed by a bully. It is also important that alleged bullies are afforded appropriate protection while complaints are considered.

---

5 Lutgen-Sandvik and Fletcher (2013) have authored an exceptionally helpful piece that sorts through the complex communal character of the bullying hornet's nest. Coming from a perspective grounded in the communication field, they explore profiles, tactics, and motivations as a framework for thinking about the larger narratives that may be presented by those involved.

Educate and train administrators in methods of response. Department chairs, deans, and other supervisors must understand that certain behaviors are not tolerated, and they should be familiar with your institution's policies and procedures for dealing with them. Ideally, these will include a set of interview questions and procedures to follow in response to complaints, all of which have been developed in consultation with your legal and human resources staff. If every complaint triggers the same institutionally required response, then the burden of exercising independent judgment is lifted, at least during the investigation period. Administrators who are conflict avoidant have a clear course of action. Improvisations are minimized. Conversations can be recorded and documented, creating a paper trail for any further actions deemed necessary.

Establish and uphold a culture where a range of perspectives and voices are heard and valued and where people are capable of calling out and responding when they see something of concern. Brodsky (1976, p. 84) argued that an organizational culture that gives a "sense of permission to harass" is one where bullying will thrive. Worse yet, once bullying is established and not rebuked in one department, it may begin to spread to others. New junior faculty coming into higher education may be better at responding if they were raised in K-12 environments that have included anti-bullying campaigns. But faculty at all levels should be encouraged and supported to develop effective response skills.

Define protocols for calling in experts. Situations of violence or serious mental illness require specific responses, such as those that may already be in place for dealing with students on your campus. Care teams and other responses designed for students can be—should be—adapted for use with faculty members and other employees as well.

You Are Not Alone

Because workplace bullying has been acknowledged more widely in recent years, there are a number of resources available. The many books, articles, and the website Workplace Bullying Institute that are the life's work of Drs. Ruth and Gary Namie are excellent places to start. Books like *Faculty Incivility* (Twale & De Luca, 2008), *Bully in the Ivory Tower* (Hollis, 2012), and foundational studies by Keashly and Neuman (2008; 2010) represent important steps forward. Several resources are designed specifically to support university administrators (Cipriano, 2011; Crookston, 2012). Leaders of faculty development centers are exploring this topic as well (De Pietro & Buddie, 2014).

Our selected Bibliography begins on page 126. These are among the resources offering insights into this vexing, costly, and demoralizing problem and helping us develop strategies for addressing it. You are not operating in a vacuum, and you are most assuredly not alone.

References

Bartlett, James E. and Michelle E. Bartlett. "Workplace Bullying: An Integrative Literature Review." *Advances in Developing Human Resources*, 13(1), 2011.

Brodsky, Carroll M. *The Harassed Worker*. Lexington, MA: D.C. Health and Company, 1976.

Cipriano, Robert. *Facilitating a Collegial Department in Higher Education: Strategies for Success*. Jossey-Bass, 2011.

Clark, Cynthia M., Lynda Olender, Diane Kenski, and Cari Cardoni. "Exploring and Addressing Faculty-to-Faculty Incivility: A National Perspective and Literature Review." *Journal of Nursing Education*, 52(4), March 2013.

Crookston, R. Kent. *Working With Problem Faculty: A Six-Step Guide for Department Chairs*. Jossey-Bass, 2013.

Di Pietro, Michele and Amy Buddie. "Academic Bullying: Leveraging Existing Research to Create More Civil Institutions." Workshop presented at the annual meeting of POD: Professional and Organizational Development in Higher Education. Dallas, TX, November 2014.

Edwards, Marissa S. and Jerald Greenberg. "What is Insidious Workplace Behavior?" *Insidious Workplace Behavior*, Jerald Greenberg, Ed. New York: Routledge, 2010.

Frood, Arran. "Death in Academia and the Mis-measurement of Science." *EuroScientist* website, February 9, 2015.

Giacalone, Robert A. and Mark D. Promislo. "Unethical and Unwell: Decrements in Well-being and Unethical Activity at Work." *Journal of Business Ethics*, 91(2), May 2009.

Hollis, Leah P. "Not Just Child's Play: Bullying and Higher Ed." *Not In Our Town* website, December 5, 2012.

Keashly, Loraleigh and Joel H. Neuman. "Faculty Experiences with Bullying in Higher Education: Causes, Consequences, and Management." *Administrative Theory & Praxis*, 32(1), September 2010.

---. "Final Report: Workplace Behavior (Bullying) Project Survey." Minnesota State University-Mankato, 2008.

Keefe, Patrick R. "A Loaded Gun: A Mass Shooter's Tragic Past." *The New Yorker*, February 11, 2013.

Lutgen-Sandvik, Pamela and C. Fletcher. "A Nasty Piece of Work: Goals and Communicative Actions of Parties in Workplace Bullying Conflicts." *Western States Communication Association*, Reno, NV; February 2013.

Namie, Gary and Ruth Namie. "WBI Survey: Workplace Bullying Health Impact." *Workplace Bullying Institute* website, August 2012.

---. *Workplace Bullying Institute* website, December 14, 2015.

---. "2014 WBI U.S. Workplace Bullying Survey." *Workplace Bullying Institute* website, February 2014.

Nielsen, Morten B., Geir H. Nielsen, Guy Notelaers, and Stale Einarsen. "Workplace Bullying and Suicidal Ideation: A 3-Wave Longitudinal Norwegian Study." *American Journal of Public Health*, 105(11), November 2015.

Petrina, Stephen, Ed. "New Workplace Issue: Academic Bullying and Mobbing." *Workplace Blog* website, Institute for Critical Education Studies, June 8, 2015.

Rayner, Charlotte, Helge Hoel, and Cary Cooper. *Workplace Bullying: What we know, who is to blame and what can we do?* Boca Raton, FL: CRC Press, November 2001.

Salin, Denise, Aino Tenhiala, Marie-Elene Roberge, and Jennifer L. Berdahl. (2014). "'I wish I had...': Target reflections on responses to workplacement mistreatment." *Human Relations*, 67(10), September 2014.

Twale, Darla and Barbara M. De Luca. *Faculty Incivility: The Rise of the Academic Bully Culture and What to Do About It.* San Francisco: Jossey Bass, 2008.

Yamada, David. "When workplace bullies claim victim status: Avoiding the judo flip." *Minding the Workplace: The New Workplace Institute* blog. May 2013.

5

Resources and Recommended Reading

Institutional Responses

By Libby Roderick

At UAA's Center for Advancing Faculty Excellence (CAFE)—as in most teaching and learning centers—we hear about the impacts of incivility, as faculty try to cope with behaviors that wreak havoc within their departments. Sometimes the chair is the bully; other times the chair is the one bullied. Sometimes there's a racial or xenophobic element: a white faculty member might bully a colleague of color or a foreign-born colleague who may even have greater academic status but less job security within a department. Sometimes staff members undermine faculty; other times, faculty treat staff like unpaid servants. Administrators sometimes engage in manipulation, secrecy, over-delegation of work, and other toxic behaviors.

Whatever form it takes, these damaging and disrespectful behaviors drain productivity and safety out of the working and learning environment and bring tremendous costs, both psychological and material. Higher education institutions are finding these costs too high to bear, and they are beginning to respond.

In *Workplace Bullying in Higher Education*, author Jamie Lester explores ethical dimensions at all four levels of the system: individual, educational, organizational, and societal. Citing a variety of sources (including Bertam et. al., 2011; Bulutlar and Oz, 2008; Cassell, 2011; LaVan and Martin, 2008; McKay et. al., 2008; Salin, 2003; and Von Bergen, 2006), she concludes that, "Workplace bullying is systemic, shaped and reinforced by forces emanating from outside the particular individuals involved." Because it is not a single negative act but "persistent, repeated, and continuous behavior…it is the system or environment that allows bullying to exist."

For most of us, the challenge will be to move from merely having policies on paper to institutionalizing clear pathways of effective response that respect academic freedom, free speech, and divergent viewpoints, identities, backgrounds, and communication styles. This will not be easy, but systemic problems demand systemic solutions. Effective responses require system-wide engagement and must include individuals at all levels of the university, from presidents and chancellors to staff and students.

Many universities, including UAA, are beginning to develop and adopt anti-bullying policies and take a variety of positive steps toward culture change. The following are a few examples.

University of Alaska Anchorage

Faculty Book Discussion Group and Recommendations

CAFE sponsored a book discussion group, led by Dr. Osama Abaza of the Engineering department (see his essay, page 99), based on the book *Facilitating a Collegial Department* by Robert Cipriano. This book includes a valuable discussion of "20 Steps Chairs Can Take" to promote collegiality within departments (pp. 56-60) as well as many other recommendations for system-wide change, including leadership strategies, codes of conduct, and interview questions to aid the faculty search process.

Faculty participants shared many thoughts on the best way to promote a collegial working environment on our UAA campus. They recommended that faculty members be encouraged to define collegiality in their various contexts and to make recommendations to academic leaders and to their unions.

The group developed the following specific recommendations for promoting collegiality within our system:

- Provide modest incentives to departments in order to create their own codes of conduct annually.
- Add additional language to the union contracts and the faculty handbook specifying what's expected of faculty, in terms of behavior, to promote a positive and professional working environment for students, colleagues, and staff.
- Develop and offer 10-minute face-to-face modules in department meetings, as well as online modules for faculty on the elements of collegiality and civility in a higher education environment (e.g., Cyberbullying and How to Prevent It; How to Create a Departmental Code of Conduct; The Elements of Professional Behavior; etc.). Use these to promote discussions within departments.
- Add questions related to civility and professional behavior to the hiring criteria/job description for hiring new faculty.
- Support training for chairs and deans every other year to increase their ability to successfully develop a collegial culture in their units.
- Develop a UAA Statement of Collegiality (or Civility), based upon examples from other universities, and include it in institution-wide documents, such as Board of Regents' policies or human resources documents that pertain to all university constituencies. This will provide academic leaders and others with a basis for discussion about collegial behavior university-wide.
- Distribute copies of Cipriano's book to faculty and administrators.

Performances and Discussions of *Toxic Friday*

CAFE hosted five live performances of *Toxic Friday* (see script and tips for staging your own production in Part 3). The performances were used to launch discussions amongst faculty and between faculty, administrators, human resources personnel and union representatives about the best next steps we can take at UAA to address this issue. CAFE also sponsored hands-on workshops in which faculty were led through a series of theater-based activities to illuminate possible ways of responding to bullying in their departments.

Led by former UAA theater faculty member Dr. Gabrielle Barnett, participants role-played specific situations they had witnessed, heard about, experienced, or feared they might experience. Exercises were structured to preserve anonymity.

Confidential Hotline for Reporting Misconduct
The University of Alaska (UA) Statewide Human Resources division has contracted with an outside third party to offer a reporting system called the UA Confidential Hotline that promises to be "a comprehensive and confidential internet and telephone based reporting tool to assist management and employees in working together to address fraud, waste, abuse, and other misconduct in the workplace, all while cultivating a positive work environment…The hotline should be used when all established avenues to fix the issue have been tried, if there is no clear reporting line, or anonymity is required by the report" (UA website). Human Resources personnel have encouraged members of the university community to use this hotline to report instances of bullying on campus; the report must be responded to within five days of receipt.

Alaska Statewide Policies

Whenever we hold discussions on this topic, we remind our participants that while we don't yet have a formal academic bullying policy, we are governed by several relevant statewide policies.

From the University of Alaska (UA) Board of Regents' Corrective Action Policy
Supervisors will apply necessary and appropriate corrective action whenever an employee fails to meet the required standards of conduct or performance. Corrective action may be necessary because of
- inability to work effectively with others;
- fighting on the job;
- acts endangering others;
- inappropriate behavior toward others; or
- harassment of others.

From the United Academics (UNAC) Collective Bargaining Agreement
6.2 Academic freedom is accompanied by the corresponding responsibility to…exercise appropriate restraint, to show respect for the opinions of others…
6.4 The UA and UNAC agree that all members of the academic community have an obligation to maintain accepted standards of civility and professionalism.

From the Alaska Code of Ethics and Teaching Standards (which governs all members of the teaching profession)
An educator…

2) shall accord just and equitable treatment of all members of the profession in the exercise of their professional rights and responsibilities

3) may not use coercive means or promise special treatment in order to influence professional decisions or colleagues

4) may not sexually harass a fellow employee

5) shall not withhold and safeguard information acquired about colleagues in the course of employment, unless disclosure serves a compelling professional purpose

7) may not deliberately misrepresent the educator's or another's professional qualifications

10) may not intentionally make a false or malicious statement about a colleague's professional performance or conduct

Eastern Washington University

From the Bullying Prevention and Response Policy
Eastern Washington University will not tolerate bullying behavior directed toward any member of the university community…

Bullying is behavior that:
- is intentional;
- is targeted at an individual or group;
- is repeated;
- is hostile or offensive; and
- creates an intimidating and/or threatening environment which produces a risk of psychological and/or physical harm.

Bullying behavior may take many forms, including, but not limited to, physical, verbal, or written acts or behaviors. It may also manifest as excluding behavior such as ignoring or dismissing individuals or groups.

Hostile behaviors include, but are not limited to, behaviors that are harmful or damaging to an individual and/or property. Behaviors that are intimidating, threatening, disruptive, humiliating, sarcastic, or vicious may also constitute hostile behavior.

Offensive behaviors may include, but are not limited to, inappropriate behaviors such as abusive language, derogatory remarks, insults, or epithets. Other offensive behaviors may include the use of condescending, humiliating, or vulgar language, swearing, shouting or use of unsuitable language, use of obscene gestures, or mocking.

Oregon State University

From the Bullying Policy

Bullying is defined as conduct of any sort directed at another that is severe, pervasive or persistent, and is of a nature that would cause a reasonable person in the victim's position substantial emotional distress and undermine his or her ability to work, study or participate in his or her regular life activities or participate in the activities of the University, and actually does cause the victim substantial emotional distress and undermines the victim's ability to work, study, or participate in the victim's regular life activities or participate in the activities of the University.

University of Wisconsin Madison

From University Committee Recommendation: language defining hostile and intimidating behavior

Unwelcome behavior that a reasonable person would find hostile and/or intimidating, and that makes the conditions for work less hospitable and does not further the University's academic or operational interest is unacceptable as it impairs another's ability to perform his/her responsibilities to the university. A person or a group can perpetrate this behavior. The person need not be more senior than or a supervisor to the target. Unacceptable behavior may include, but is not limited to:

- Abusive expression (including spoken, written, recorded, visual, digital, or nonverbal, etc.) directed at another person in the workplace, such as derogatory remarks or epithets that are outside the range of commonly accepted expressions of disagreement, disapproval, or critique in an academic culture and professional setting that respects free expression;
- Unwarranted physical contact or intimidating gestures;
- Exclusion or isolation having the effect of harming another person's reputation in the workplace or hindering another person's work;
- Sabotage of another person's work or impeding another person's capacity for academic expression, be it oral, written, or other;
- Abuse of authority, such as using threats or retaliation in the exercise of authority, supervision, or guidance, or impeding another person from exercising shared governance rights, etc.;
- Repeated acts or a pattern of hostile and/or intimidating behaviors are of particular concern. A single act typically will not be sufficient to warrant discipline or dismissal, but an especially severe or egregious act may warrant either.

This definition…is not intended to impede academic freedom or violate rights to free expression. It is intended, rather, to foster a workplace that ensures all persons the exercise of these rights…

Other Resources

Anti-Bullying Workshops, Objective Mediators

In an online article for the American Association of University Professors ("Prevention of Bullying on Campus"), Clara Wajngurt makes the following recommendations:

> Colleges and universities can arrange an early-alert program in which administrative and academic departments are trained to recognize workplace bullying. In addition to educating faculty and staff on harassment policies, institutions can offer workshops on anti-bullying behavior. An objective mediator or someone who specializes in conflict resolution can also be helpful, since people who are being bullied often cannot confront the bullies themselves. Grievances over alleged bullying behavior must be taken seriously.
>
> An effective policy should help employees understand what steps to take in response to inappropriate behavior at work and what behavior is expected of employees. It should also describe the steps for filing a complaint and provide for the involvement of a third party well versed in aggression, control, conflict, and resolution to support the victim.

Care Teams or Ombudspeople for Faculty

Most universities now offer some version of a care team for students that provides suicide prevention services, support for individuals with challenges, and interventions involving problematic behavior. UAA's care team provides "consultation and support to faculty, staff, administrators, and students in assisting individuals who display concerning or disruptive behaviors." Other care teams may respond specifically to faculty-on-faculty situations. You might also choose to designate a particular individual to serve as ombudsperson in colleague-to-colleague bullying situations.

Assessment Materials

Colleges and universities need to evaluate collegiality in a fair, objective, and reproducible manner to avoid the very real potential for accusations of "incivility" by administrators or colleagues with questionable political agendas. Jeffrey L. Buller and Robert E. Cipriano have created two assessment instruments designed to help take the subjectivity out of evaluations of faculty collegiality.

- The Collegiality Assessment Matrix (CAM) identifies and measures observable behaviors that are commonly associated with collegiality in academic settings (e.g., displays of anger or irritability, contemptuous or dismissive conduct, failing to "step up" and serve when needed, etc.). The instrument allows faculty members and administrators to rate one another.
- The Self-Assessment Matrix (S-AM) is a similar instrument that allows faculty members to rate themselves.

Dual ratings would make it possible for department chairs and deans to point to differences in perception as a basis for discussion with individual faculty members. These instruments can be used on a regular basis in faculty performance reviews, in tenure and promotion evaluations, and in post-tenure reviews. They are commercial products that can be ordered directly from Atlas Leadership.

Bibliography

The reading list below is by no means definitive or complete. Academic bullying is a relatively new field of inquiry, and the body of research continues to grow. Many materials are currently available only in blogs and on-line forums; some are associated with professional journals while others lean toward the self-help and behavioral therapy end of the spectrum. We have included in the following list all the sources cited by our contributors, plus recommendations for further reading.

Anonymous academics. "Bullying in academia: 'Professors are supposed to be stressed! That's the job.'" *The Guardian*, Higher Education Network. October 24, 2014.

Azziz, Ricardo. "Back to the Future: Why Is the Diversity of University Leadership Stuck in the '80s?" *Huffington Post*, June 24, 2014.

Banaji, Mahzarin R. and Anthony G. Greenwald. *Blind Spot: Hidden Biases of Good People.* New York: Delacorte Press, 2013.

Bartlett, James E. and Michelle E. Bartlett. "Workplace Bullying: An Integrative Literature Review." *Advances in Developing Human Resources*, 13(1), 2011.

Benoit, Suzanne. "Surviving a Toxic Workplace Without Losing Your Mind." *Benoit Consulting* website, November 7, 2011.

Brodsky, Carroll M. *The Harassed Worker.* Lexington, MA: D.C. Health and Company, 1976.

Buller, Jeffrey L. *The Essential Department Chair: A Practical Guide to College Administration.* Bolton, MA: Anker Publishing, 2006.

Buller, Jeffrey L. and Robert E. Cipriano. "The CAM and S-AM." ATLAS: *Leadership Training for Higher Education* website, 2013.

Burton, James P. and Jenny M. Hoobler. "Subordinate self-esteem and abusive supervision." Pittsburg State University: *Journal of Managerial Issues*, 2006.

Cassell, Macgorine. "Bullying in Academe: Prevalent, Significant, and Incessant." Fairmont State University: *Contemporary Issues in Education Research,* May 2011.

Chernoff, Marc, Angel Chernoff and Kathy Caprino. "12 Toxic Behaviors That Push People Away From You." *The Open Mind* website, March 17, 2015.

Chu, Don. *The Department Chair Primer: What Chairs Need to Know and Do to Make a Difference.* Jossey Bass, 2012.

Cipriano, Robert. *Facilitating a Collegial Department in Higher Education: Strategies for Success.* Jossey-Bass, 2011.

Clark, Cynthia M., Lynda Olender, Diane Kenski, and Cari Cardoni. "Exploring and Addressing Faculty-to-Faculty Incivility: A National Perspective and Literature Review." *Journal of Nursing Education,* 52(4), March 2013.

Crookston, R. Kent. *Working With Problem Faculty: A 6-Step Guide for Department Chairs.* Jossey-Bass, 2012.

David, E. J. R., & Annie O. Derthick. "What is internalized oppression, and so what?" *Internalized Oppression: The Psychology of Marginalized Groups.* E.J.R. David, Editor. New York: Springer Publishing, 2014.

de Becker, Gavin. *The Gift of Fear: And Other Survival Signals That Protect Us from Violence.* New York: Dell, 1999.

De Luca, Barbara M. and Darla J. Twale. "Mediating in the Academic Bully Culture: The Chair's Responsibility to Faculty and Graduate Students." *The Department Chair: A Resource for Academic Administrators,* 20 (3), Winter 2010. Retrieved from Tomorrow's Professor Mailing List (Message #992), Stanford Center for Teaching and Learning.

Duffy, Michelle K. and Walter Ferrier. "Birds of a feather…How supervisor-subordinate dissimilarity moderates the influence of supervisor behaviors on workplace attitudes." *Group and Organizational Management,* 28(2), June 2003.

Eastern Washington University Board of Trustees. "Bullying Prevention and Response." EWU Policy 901-04, Rev. 2010.

Edwards, Marissa S. and Jerald Greenberg. "What is Insidious Workplace Behavior?" *Insidious Workplace Behavior,* Jerald Greenberg, Ed. New York: Routledge, 2010.

Farley, Sam and Christine Sprigg. "Culture of cruelty: why bullying thrives in higher education." *The Guardian,* Higher Education Network, November 3, 2014.

Farrington, Elizabeth Leigh. "Bullying on Campus: How to Identify, Prevent, Resolve It." *Women in Higher Education,* 19(3), March 2010. Wiley On-Line Library, May 9, 2014.

Fogg, Piper. "Academic Bullies: The Web provides new outlets for aggression." *The Chronicle of Higher Education* website, September 12, 2008.

Frood, Arran. "Death in Academia and the Mis-measurement of Science." *EuroScientist* website, February 9, 2015.

Geddes, Deanna and Lisa T. Stickney. "The trouble with sanctions: Organizational responses to deviant anger displays at work." *Human Relations,* 64(2), February 2011.

Giacalone, Robert A. and Mark D. Promislo. "Unethical and Unwell: Decrements in Well-being and Unethical Activity at Work." *Journal of Business Ethics,* 91(2), May 2009.

Gillespie, Nicole, M. Walsh, Anthony H. Winefield, Jagdish Dua, and Con K.K. Stough. "Occupational Stress in Universities: Staff Perceptions of the Causes, Consequences and Moderators of Stress." *Work and Stress,* 15(1), 2001.

Gravois, John. "Mob Rule: In departmental disputes, professors can act just like animals." *Chronicle of Higher Education*, April 2006.

Greenberg, Jerald and Jason Colquitt. *Handbook of Organizational Justice*. Lawrence Erlbaum Associates, 2005.

Harlos, Karen. "If you build a remedial voice mechanism, will they come? Determinants of voicing interpersonal mistreatment at work." *Human Relations*, 63(3), January 2010.

Higgerson, Mary Lou and Teddi A. Joyce. *Effective Leadership Communication: A Guide For Department Chairs And Deans For Managing Difficult Situations And People*. Bolton, MA: Anker Publishing Company, 2007.

Hollis, Leah. P. *Bully in the Ivory Tower: How Aggression and Incivility Erode American Higher Education*. New York: Berkley Books, 2012.

---. "Not Just Child's Play: Bullying and Higher Ed." *Not In Our Town* website, December 5, 2012.

Keashly, Loraleigh and Joel H. Neuman. "Bullying in academia: What does current theorizing and research tell us?" *Workplace Bullying in Higher Education: Causes, Consequences, and Management*. Jamie Lester, Ed. New York: Routledge, 2013.

---. "Faculty Experiences with Bullying in Higher Education: Causes, Consequences, and Management." *Administrative Theory & Praxis*, 32(1), September 2010.

---. "Final Report: Workplace Behavior (Bullying) Project Survey." Minnesota State University-Mankato, 2008.

Keefe, Patrick R. "A Loaded Gun: A Mass Shooter's Tragic Past." *The New Yorker*, February 11, 2013.

Lampman, Claudia, Alissa Phelps, Samantha Bancroft, and Melissa Beneke. "Contrapower Harassment in Academia: A Survey of Faculty Experience with Student Incivility, Bullying, and Sexual Attention." *Sex Roles: A Journal of Research*, 60(5), March 2009.

Lampman, Claudia. "Women Faculty at Risk: U.S. Professors Report on Their Experiences with Student Incivility, Bullying, Aggession, and Sexual Attention." *NASPA Journal About Women in Higher Education*, 5, 2012.

Lassila, Kathrin Day. "Race, Speech and Values: What really happened at Yale." *Yale Alumni Magazine*, Jan/Feb 2016.

Lee, Barbara A. and Peter H. Ruger. *Accomodating Faculty and Staff with Psychiatric Disabilities*. Washington DC: National Association of College and University Attorneys, 1997.

Lester, Jaime. "Not Your Child's Playground: Workplace Bullying Among Community College Faculty." *Community College Journal of Research and Practice*, 33(5), 2009.

Lester, Jaime, Ed. *Workplace Bullying in Higher Education*. New York: Routledge, 2013.

Lutgen-Sandvik, Pamela and C. Fletcher. "A Nasty Piece of Work: Goals and Communicative Actions of Parties in Workplace Bullying Conflicts." *Western States Communication Association,* Reno, NV; February 2013.

McKay, Ruth, Diane H. Arnold, Jae Fratzl, and Roland Thomas. "Workplace Bullying in Academia: A Canadian Study." *Employee Responsibilities and Rights Journal,* 20(2), 2008.

Mewburn, Inger, Ed. "Academic assholes and the circle of niceness." *The Thesis Whisperer,* February 2013.

Namie, Gary. "U.S. Hostile Workplace Survey 2000." *Workplace Bullying Institute* website, 2008.

---. "U.S. Workplace Bullying Survey." Workplace Bullying Institute and Zogby International, September 2007.

Namie, Gary and Ruth Namie. *The Bully at Work: What You Can Do to Stop the Hurt and Reclaim your Dignity on the Job.* 2nd edition. Naperville, IL: Sourcebooks, 2009.

---. *The Bully-free Workplace: Stop Jerks, Weasels, and Snakes from Ruining your Organization.* Hoboken, NJ: Wiley, 2011.

---. *Workplace Bullying Institute* website.

---. "2014 WBI U.S. Workplace Bullying Survey." *Workplace Bullying Institute* website, February 2014.

Nelson, Cary. "Defining Academic Freedom." *Inside Higher Ed,* December 21, 2010.

Nielsen, Morten B., Geir H. Nielsen, Guy Notelaers, and Stale Einarsen. "Workplace Bullying and Suicidal Ideation: A 3-Wave Longitudinal Norwegian Study." *American Journal of Public Health,* 105(11), November 2015.

Oregon State University Office of Equity and Inclusion. "Oregon State University Bullying Policy." 2013.

Oxenford, Carolyn B. and Sally L. Kuhlenschmidt. "Working Effectively with Psychologically Impaired Faculty." *To Improve the Academy (Volume 30),* Judith E. Miller and James E. Groccia, Eds. Jossey-Bass, 2011.

Patterson, Kerry, Joseph Grenny, Ron McMillan, and Al Switzler. *Crucial Conversations: Tools for Talking When Stakes are High.* 2nd Ed. McGraw Hill, 2013.

Patterson, Kerry, Joseph Grenny, Ron McMillan, Al Switzler, and David Maxfield. *Crucial Accountability: Tools for Resolving Violated Expectations, Broken Commitments, and Bad Behavior.* 2nd Ed. McGraw Hill Education, June 2013.

Petrina, Stephen, Ed. "New Workplace Issue: Academic Bullying and Mobbing." *Workplace Blog* website, Institute for Critical Education Studies, June 8, 2015.

Prilleltensky, Isaac and Lev Gonick. "Polities Change, Oppression Remains: On the Psychology and Politics of Oppression." *International Society of Political Psychology,* 17, March 1996.

Proudhon, Pierre-Joseph. "Faculty Experiences with Bullying in Higher Education: Causes, Consequences, and Management." *Bullying of Faculty in Higher Education* blogspot, September 23, 2010.

---. "Faculty Experiences with Bullying in Higher Education: Causes, Consequences, and Management." *Bullying of Faculty in Higher Education* blogspot, December 16, 2010.

Rayner, Charlotte, Helge Hoel, and Cary Cooper. *Workplace Bullying: What we know, who is to blame and what can we do?* Boca Raton, FL: CRC Press, November 2001.

Rivera, David. "Bullying and Microaggressions. Bullying: More than physical violence." *Psychology Today,* January 23, 2011.

Ruark, Jennifer. "In Academic Culture, Mental-Health Problems Are Hard to Recognize and Hard to Treat." *Chronicle of Higher Education,* February 16, 2010.

Safety and Health Assessment and Research for Prevention program. "Workplace Bullying and Disruptive Behavior: What Everyone Needs to Know." Washington State Department of Labor and Industries, 87-2-2011, April 2011.

Salin, Denise, Aino Tenhiala, Marie-Elene Roberge, and Jennifer L. Berdahl. (2014). "'I wish I had…': Target reflections on responses to workplace mistreatment." *Human Relations,* 67(10), September 2014.

Schwebel, David. "Impaired Faculty: Helping Academics Who Are Suffering From Serious Mental Illness." *Academic Leadership,* 7(2), April 2009.

Schnieder, Pat. "UW-Madison professor worried that anti-bullying policy will stifle speech." *The Capital Times,* January 21, 2015.

Stone, William D. "Bullying Prevention Program: Possible Impact on Academic Performance." *Doctoral Dissertations and Projects,* Paper 145, Liberty University, 2009.

Sue, Derald Wing, Editor. *Microaggressions and Marginality: Manifestations, Dynamics, and Impact.* Hoboken, New Jersey: John Wiley and Sons, 2010.

Taylor, Susan. "Workplace Bullying in Higher Education: Faculty Experiences and Responses." Dissertation, University of Minnesota, 2012.

Tepper , Bennett J. "Consequences of Abusive Supervision." *The Academy of Management,* 43(2), April 2000.

Tepper, Bennett J, Michelle K. Duffy, Jenny Hoobler, and Michael D. Ensley. "Moderators of the Relationships Between Coworkers' Organizational Citizenship Behavior and Fellow Employees' Attitudes." *Journal of Applied Psychology,* 89(3), July 2004.

Twale, Darla and Barbara M. De Luca. *Faculty Incivility: The Rise of the Academic Bully Culture and What to Do About It*. San Francisco: Jossey Bass, 2008.

University of Alaska Anchorage. "UAA Faculty and Staff Insight Survey." Conducted November 2012. UAA website, Undergraduate Academic Affairs.

University of Wisconsin Madison. "University Committee Recommendations to Add Section II-332 to Faculty Legislation Defining Language Describing Hostile and/or Intimidating Behavior." Faculty Document 2511, 2014.

Von Bergen, C.W., J.A. Zavaletta, Jr., and B. Soper. "Legal Remedies for Workplace Bullying: Grabbing the Bully by the Horns." *Employee Relations Law Journal*, Vol. 32, 2006.

Westhues, Kenneth et al. *The Remedy and Prevention of Mobbing in Higher Education: Two Case Studies*. Lewiston, NY: The Edwin Mellen Press, 2006.

Yamada, David. "When Workplace Bullies Claim Victim Status: Avoiding the Judo Flip." *Minding the Workplace: The New Workplace Institute* blog. May 2013.

---. "Workplace Bullying and Mobbing in Academe: The Hell of Heaven?" *Minding the Workplace: The New Workplace Institute* blog. Revised April 9, 2014.

Noteworthy Websites and Blogs

Bullying of Faculty in Higher Education. Pierre-Joseph Proudhon.

Historiann. Ann M. Little.

The Mobbing Portal. Kenneth Westhuis, University of Waterloo, Ontario.

On Hiring. Chronicle of Higher Education.

The Workplace Bullying Institute. Gary Namie and Ruth Namie.

Resources for Responding to Active Bullying Situations

Comaford, Christine. "How to Stop Workplace Bullies In Their Tracks." *Forbes*, March 12, 2014.

Curry, Lynne. *Beating the Workplace Bully: A Tactical Guide to Taking Charge*. American Management Association: AMACOM Books, 2016.

Namie, Gary and Ruth Namie. "The WBI 3-Step Target Action Plan: What Bullied Targets Can Do." *The Workplace Bullying Institute* website.

Scivicque, Chrissy. "5 Steps for Handling a Workplace Bully." *U.S. News & World Report*, Jan. 24, 2013.

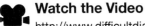
Watch the Video
http://www.difficultdialoguesuaa.org/toxicfriday/
Username: toxicfriday
Password: t0xiC*!#

Video Credits

Toxic Friday: the Video
Producer: Libby Roderick
Director: Mary Katzke, Affinity Films
Rehearsal Director: Dr. Gabrielle Barnett
Scriptwriter: Dr. Andréa J. Onstad

Cast, in order of appearance
Rachel: Jane Henriksen Baird
Simon: Todd Sherwood
Charles: Peter Porco
Emily: Mariyam Medovaya
Carol: Vivian Melde
Dean Stone: Joan Cullinane
Talkback Emcee: Julia Cossman

Audience members
Greta Artman
Gabrielle Barnett
John Dede
Steve Johnson
Lynn Koshiyama
Rebeca Maseda
Ilarion (Larry) Merculieff
Terry Nelson
Paul Ongtooguk
Libby Roderick
Blade Smithee
Shawnalee Whitney

Development Assistance
Libby Roderick
Dr. Gabrielle Barnett
Dr. Suzanne Burgoyne

Faculty and staff of
University of Alaska Anchorage
University of Missouri
University of Texas, Austin

Actors
Jane Henriksen Baird
Joan Cullinane
Tami Lubitsh
Jerry McDonnell
John McKay
Vivian Melde
Nava Saracino
Todd Sherwood
Kelly Lee Williams

Filmed in May 2015 at the
Journalism TV Studio,
University of Alaska Anchorage

Copyright 2015 by the University of Alaska
Anchorage
Thomas Case, Chancellor
3211 Providence Drive
Anchorage AK 99508

Characters and material are fictitious.
Resemblance to any persons, living or dead,
is strictly coincidental.

Thanks to

Paola Banchero
Associate Professor and Department Chair
Journalism and Communication

Renee Carter-Chapman
Senior Vice Provost
Office of Institutional Effectiveness, Engagement
and Academic Support

John Dede
Special Assistant
Office of Institutional Effectiveness, Engagement
and Academic Support

Liisa Morrison
Program Manager
Center for Advancing Faculty Excellence

Shawnalee Whitney
Interim Director
Center for Advancing Faculty Excellence

Sam Zeller
Studio Manager
Department of Journalism and Communications

Special Thanks to

Dr. Suzanne Burgoyne
Curators' Distinguished Teaching Professor of
Theatre
Director, Center for Applied Theatre and
Drama Research
University of Missouri

Cyrano's Theater Company
Anchorage, Alaska

Spontaneous Co-Motion
Anchorage, Alaska

With support from

United Academics

University of Alaska Anchorage (UAA)
- Difficult Dialogues Initiative
- Facilities and Campus Services/Environmental
  Health and Safety/Risk Management
- Office of the Provost
- Center for Advancing Faculty Excellence (CAFE)
- Office of Institutional Effectiveness,
  Engagement and Academic Support (IEEAS)
- Department of Journalism and
  Communication

Alaska Airlines

Difficult Dialogues at UAA

www.difficultdialoguesuaa.org

UAA's Difficult Dialogues Initiative is an outgrowth of the Ford Foundation's national Difficult Dialogue program launched in 2005 to promote academic freedom and religious, cultural, and political pluralism on college and university campuses.

In a unique partnership between a public and private university, UAA and neighboring Alaska Pacific University (APU) jointly launched two tracks of faculty development work designed to

- build the skills, networks, and confidence to cultivate learning environments in which all viewpoints are respected and civil discourse is modeled and taught;
- develop learning climates that are more inclusive of minority voices/ways of knowing and safer places for the free exchange of ideas; and
- cultivate deeper understandings between Alaska's Native and academic communities.

The Engaging Controversy track included
- weeklong faculty development intensives aimed at increasing skill levels for introducing difficult dialogues into the classroom;
- a Books of the Year program, in which texts addressing controversial issues are discussed in classrooms and the community; and
- the creation of *Start Talking: A Handbook for Engaging Controversial Topics in Higher Education*, a nationally acclaimed field manual which describes the UAA/APU model, shares the experiences of program participants, and describes strategies for classroom use.

The Alaska Native Ways of Teaching and Learning track included
- a weeklong faculty development intensive that introduced traditional Alaska Native "best practices" for teaching and learning as well as key difficult dialogues between indigenous and academic communities;
- the creation of e-portfolios detailing faculty efforts to apply these new ways of teaching in their classrooms; and
- the creation of *Stop Talking: Indigenous Ways of Teaching and Learning and Difficult Dialogues in Higher Education*, which describes the model for a Native-designed and run faculty development intensive, strategies for applying indigenous pedagogies in western learning environments, reflections on education by Alaska Native Elders, and reports from participants on what they learned and tried in their classrooms.

Ongoing Activities

Faculty Learning Communities: semester-long discussion groups organized around the *Start Talking* and *Stop Talking* books that equip faculty to apply Difficult Dialogues strategies and indigenous teaching practices in their classrooms.

Public Policy Debates and Faculty Forums: once-a-semester facilitated public discussions that draw on UAA faculty experts and student debaters.

Books of the Year program: coordinated discussions and projects for faculty, students, staff, and community members to address faculty-selected topics of local and international significance.

Difficult Dialogues courses: courses that intentionally combine academic content with processes for engaging in respectful dialogue between participants with differing viewpoints.

Workshops: specific events for faculty, staff, and teaching assistants at UAA's community campuses.

Beyond UAA

Website: UAA's Difficult Dialogues website (www.difficultdialoguesuaa.org) contains information about a wide range of Difficult Dialogues strategies, programs, and projects throughout the U.S. and beyond; free access to two Difficult Dialogues books; and much more.

Workshops and Presentations: UAA facilitators have made presentations and conducted training sessions at a wide range of conferences and universities throughout the country, including Tufts University, the University of Wisconsin, the University of Texas at Austin, Michigan State University, Oregon State University, the University of Virginia, Oklahoma State University, and the University of Missouri.

International Partnership: UAA has partnered with South Africa's Institute for Reconciliation and Social Justice and the Centre for Teaching and Learning at the University of the Free State (UFS) in Bloemfontein to help design and deliver weeklong faculty development intensives based on the model described in the *Start Talking* book. The UFS Difficult Dialogues program now involves year-long faculty learning communities, yearly training for new students, two-day introductory trainings for new faculty, and two-day trainings for advanced faculty.

Alaskan and U.S. Partnerships: UAA has partnered with or presented to various community groups to assist in the design and facilitation of difficult dialogues of importance to Alaskan and U.S. communities. Examples include a community chorus whose members were deeply divided over the performance of Leonard Bernstein's "Mass"; First Alaskans

Institute, an indigenous policy institute, as part of its Kellogg grant to develop a movement for racial equity in Alaska; and One Earth, One People, a group of religious leaders, Alaska Native Elders, and climate scientists seeking to stimulate conversation about moral elements of the climate crisis.

Difficult Dialogues National Resource Center (DDNRC): Libby Roderick, UAA's Difficult Dialogues Director, serves as Vice President for the DDNRC, a consortium of institutions and individuals committed to advancing meaningful Difficult Dialogues practices in higher education.

National Recognition: UAA was cited as an exemplar by the editors of *Pluralism and Academic Freedom: Promising Practices and Lessons Learned from the Difficult Dialogues Initiative* (Hernandez-Gravelle, O'Neill, and Batten, Eds. Charlottesville, Va.: Thomas Jefferson Center for the Protection of Free Expression, 2012).

Publications

Landis, Kay, Ed. S*tart Talking: A Handbook for Engaging Difficult Dialogues in Higher Education*. University of Alaska Anchorage, 2008.

Merculieff, Ilarion and Libby Roderick. *Stop Talking: Indigenous Ways of Teaching and Learning and Difficult Dialogues in Higher Education*. University of Alaska Anchorage, 2013.

Roderick, Libby, Ed. *Alaska Native Cultures and Issues: Responses to Frequently Asked Questions*. 2nd Ed. University of Alaska Press, 2010.

Roderick, Libby. "Difficult Dialogues and Transformational Change through Cross-Cultural Faculty Development." *To Improve the Academy*, Vol. 30. Jossey-Bass, October 2011.

Acknowledgements

The editor wishes to thank the following
individuals for their generosity in reading
this project in manuscript form and for their
valuable observations and comments:

Raymond Anthony
Lauren Bruce
Renee Carter-Chapman
Jack Curtiss
John Dede
Sheri Denison
Christina Gheen
Sara Juday
Judith Owens-Manley
Jack Roderick
Karen Roth

CPSIA information can be obtained
at www.ICGtesting.com
Printed in the USA
FSOW03n0456280616
22070FS